CAMBRIDGESHIRE
Place-Names

Published by Sigma Leisure – an imprint of Sigma Press, Stobart House, Pontyclerc, Penybanc Road, Ammanford, Carmarthenshire SA18 3HP.

British Library Cataloguing in Publication Data
A CIP record for this book is available from the British Library.

ISBN: 978-1-85058-959-4

Typesetting and Design by: Sigma Press, Ammanford, Carmarthenshire

Cover photographs:

Photographs: © Anthony Poulton-Smith

Printed by: TJ International Ltd, Padstow, Cornwall

Disclaimer: the information in this book is given in good faith and is believed to be correct at the time of publication. No responsibility is accepted by either the author or publisher for errors or omissions.

CAMBRIDGESHIRE
Place-Names

Anthony Poulton-Smith

Contents

Introduction

For years the history of England relied heavily on information from the Roman occupation. In recent years we have come to realise British history did not start with the Empire, indeed there was already a thriving culture in England well before the birth of Christ. When the Romans left our shores in the fifth century the arrival of the Anglo-Saxons was thought to herald a time of turmoil, the so-called Dark Ages. Yet they brought the culture and language which formed the basis of modern England with the later arrival of the Norsemen adding their own influences. The same is true of our place names, the vast majority of settlement names in Cambridgeshire are derived from Saxon or Old English, while a smattering of Old Scandinavian is also found but not as often as we would expect for a county this far east. There are also the topographical features such as rivers and hills still with names given to them by the Celts of the pre-Roman era.

Ostensibly place names are simply descriptions of the location, maybe with the addition of how it was utilised or of those living there. In these pages an examination of the origins, derivations and meanings of Cambridgeshire place names will reveal all. Not only will we see Saxon and Scandinavian settlements, but Celtic rivers, Roman roads and even Norman French landlords who have all contributed to some degree to the names with wich we are so familiar.

Not only are the basic names discussed but also districts, hills, streams, fields, roads, lanes, streets and public houses. Road and street names are normally of more recent derivation, named after those who played a significant role in the development of a town or revealing what could be seen in the landscape before the developers wiped the land clean. Businessmen and benefactors who provided housing and employment in the eighteenth and nineteenth centuries are often forgotten, yet their names live on in the sign at the end of the street and often have a story to tell. Pub names are almost a language of their own. Again they are not named arbitrarily but are based on the history of the place and can open a new window on the history of our towns and villages.

Defining place names of all varieties can give an insight into history which would otherwise be ignored or even lost. Indeed toponomy, the study of place names, is becoming an increasingly valuable tool for archaeologists and historians as more and more of our history is buried beneath a shield of concrete.

In the ensuing pages we shall examine 2,000 plus years of Cambridgeshire history. While driving around the county the author was delighted by the quintessentially English place names in the area and so, having already taken a look at several other counties turned to Cambridgeshire. This book is the result of the author's long interest in place names which has developed over many years and in many ways and which continue to intrigue and surprise.

To all who helped in some way, the librarians who aided me in my research, those who offered a place to rest, and the many who pointed a lost traveller in the right direction, a big thank you.

Place-Names

(in alphabetic order)

A

Abbotsley

The earliest surviving record of this name is as Adbolesle in the twelfth century. Here the Saxon personal name is followed by the Old English *leah* and describes 'the woodland clearing of Eadbald'.

The public house named the Eight Bells refers to the number of bells in the peal. Another we would expect to show the close association between parish church and local pub here is the Jolly Abbot, although here it is actually derived from the name of the place which ironically has nothing to do with the church.

The village has an annual Scarecrow Festival, a fundraising event for the upkeep of the village hall.

Abington (Great and Little)

A name recorded as Abintone in Domesday, it comes from Old English *ing tun* with a Saxon personal name – thus giving 'the farmstead associated with a man called Abba'. The two places have additions for distinction with obvious meaning, furthermore one undoubtedly grew from the other and hence the sharing of the name.

Locally the name of Layden's Grove was associated with the Lagden family by 1724.

Abington Pigotts

As with the previous name this is 'the farmstead associated with a man called Abba'. However as this place is fifteen miles away, and thus further than many individuals would ever travel in their entire lifetimes, it is highly unlikely to represent the same person but simply a common personal name. The addition here is a reference to the lords of the manor, the Pykot family known to be here by the fifteenth century.

Locally we find Bibles Grove, nothing religious here this was simply home to Richard le Byboys in 1274; Alexander le Moyne was living at Moynes Manor House in 1236; and Boy Bridge was almost certainly named after the users rather than the builders.

Ailsworth

A name recorded as Aegeleswurth in 948 and as Eglesworde in 1086. Here the Saxon personal name combines with Old English *worth* and describes 'Aegel's enclosure'.

Akeman Street

This is not the original Akeman Street, this Roman road gets its name as it has been transferred from the real Roman road. Four named roads were given protection under a law passed by William the Conqueror: Watling Street, Ermine Street, Ickneild Way and the original Akeman Street. Should the rule be broken the punishment could be most severe. The original name means 'the Roman road associated with a man called Acemann', which comes from *Acemannes ceastre* and is an alternative name for the city of Bath dating from the tenth century.

Clearly the meaning of a transferred name has no significance here, unlike the thirteenth century record which shows that at least one part of this road was once known in Old English as *fyrdman* 'the soldier's way'. A further section of this route is known as Mereways, from Old English *maere weg* it describes 'the boundary way', where the path follows the line of a parish boundary.

Alconbury

Domesday gives this as Acumesberie, while by the twelfth century this is Alcumundesberia. Here the suffix is from Old English *burh* and describing 'Ealhmund's stronghold'.

Aldreth

The earliest surviving record of this name is as Alrehetha in 1170, the name derived from Old English *alor hyth* and meaning 'the landing place by the alder trees'.

Here we also find Foulmire Fen which might be describing 'the foul muddy pool', although there is a chance the first element represents *fugol* and thus 'the pool of the wild birds'. Hinton Hall seems to be from 'Hean's tun or farmstead', Linden End tells us it was 'the hill where flax is grown', Granger's Drove was associated with Samuel Granger by 1669, Salmon's Farm was home to the family of John Salmon by 1819, and Oliver Setchell was working Setchell's Farm by 1840.

The village of Aldreth was the site of two battles, at a time when Hereward the Wake fronted the Saxon fight against the Normans of William the Conqueror. It also gave its name to one of the ancient causeways through the fenland leading to the Isle of Ely.

Alwalton

Saxon personal names are often difficult to tie down with any certainty. This is hardly surprising. Indeed in fifteen centuries will our descendants ever be able to decipher the differences between Michael, Mickey, Mitchell, Mick, Mike, or even the feminine versions of Michelle and Michaela? Hence here we need to define Alwalton as 'the farmstead associated with a man called Aethelwald', or similar, with the place name recorded as Aethelwoldingtun in 955 and Alwoltune in 1086.

The village is both the birthplace (27th March 1863) and last resting place (22nd April 1933) of Sir Henry Royce, co-founder of the Rolls Royce company. Son of James and Mary (nee King), Henry was the youngest of five children who ran a flour mill leased from the Ecclesiastical Commissioners. However the business failed and they were forced to move to London to seek employment. Sadly in 1872 father James Royce died and, with only a single year of education behind him, Henry was forced out to work selling newspapers and delivering telegrams. Eventually he was introduced to engineering and so began an apprenticeship with the Great Northern Railway Company, then on to a firm of tool makers in Leeds, on to the Electric Light and Power Company, later setting up his own company in Manchester. He produced his first cars in 1902 and, with only two vehicles completed, signed the famous partnership with Charles Rolls in 1904.

Arrington

Listings of this name include Domesday's Erningtune and the earlier mid-tenth century record of Earnningtone. This is probably derived from 'the farmstead of the family or followers of Earna', with the Saxon personal name followed by Old English *inga tun*.

The family of James Wragg were associated with Wragg's Farm by 1840; while Decoy Farm and Decoy Pond, clearly a place where it was hoped to attract wildfowl, cannot have been named before the nineteenth century for this Dutch loaned word was unknown in English before this time.

Ashley

A very common place name and, as with all common names, one which comes from the simplest of origins in 'the woodland clearing of or by the ash trees'. This name comes from Old English *aesc leah* and is recorded as Esselie in Domesday and as Asshelelee in 1260.

Fielden Way is an old road, its name telling us it leads past 'the open land'. Old Suffolk Road marks the traditional boundary between Cambridgeshire and neighbouring Suffolk. Silverley is seen as Seuerlai in 1086, Silverlegh in 1195, and as Suluerleye in 1285, this comes Old English *seolfor leah* refers to 'the woodland clearing growing with silver-weed or silver-wort'.

Former inhabitants of Ashley left their mark on the map in such names as Geyons, which in 1295 it was home to John de Gynes, Houghton Farm was worked by the Houghton family in 1815, Rayner's Farm associated with William Rayner in 1815, however Duke's Farm is not a family name but was named from the landowner, the Duke of Rutland.

Ashwell Street

An ancient route which is found as Aswellestrate in 1274 and Eswelle State in 1508, a name which describes 'the hillside way'.

B

Babraham

As with many English place names this is comprised of a Saxon personal name with an Old English suffix, in this case *ham*. Recorded as Badburgham in 1086, here is 'the homestead of a woman called Beaduburh'.

Local names include Copley Hill, speaking of 'the rounded tumulus', while the last remaining sign of the old signalling station is that of the name of Signal Hill Plantation.

In the nineteenth century the village was home to Jonas Webb, a noted stock breeder whose efforts resulted in developing the breed of sheep known as the Southdown. It is also the setting for F. L. Lucas's 1938 novel *Doctor Dido*.

Bainton

The earliest surviving record of this name is as Badingtun in 980. Here the Saxon personal name is followed by the Old English *ing tun* and describes 'the farmstead associated with a man called Bada'.

Balsham

A name recorded as Bellesham in 974 and as Belesham in the Domesday survey of 1086, it comes from Old English *ham* after a Saxon personal name - thus giving 'the homestead of a man called Baelli'.

Minor names here includes Frogs Hall, either a swamp, and thus a haven for frogs, or it could be named after one Hugh Frogg who was here by 1356. As it is unclear which version came first it is impossible to say which is the true origin.

The Black Bull has numerous meanings, although if we can find first use of the name it would be a good clue, yet it is almost impossible to be certain for even when the document refers to the building of the establishment it could simply be a rebuild or extension. Here the earliest are religious, a reference to a papal bull and thus a Catholic house; later it could be an heraldic reference, although it is virtually impossible to know where it comes from as this strong imagery is quite popular; and the most modern names refer to the animal, still highly prized. The Bell is a common name for a pub, a reminder of the close traditional links between the only two meeting places for the community, the pub and the church.

The sign on the village green depicts one man. When this place was utterly destroyed in a Viking raid of 1010, it was held that just one man survived this fearful attack.

Barham

Derived from Old English *beorg ham* and recorded as Bercheham in 1086, this describes itself as 'the farmstead on a hill'.

Barnack

Here is an Old English place name from *beorn ac* and recorded as Beornican in 980 and Bernac in 1086. This name seems to describe 'the place at the oak trees associated with the warriors'.

Barrington

Domesday lists this name as Barentone, a name taking a Saxon personal name and adding Old English *tun* to refer to 'Bara's farmstead'.

One local road has the unusual name of Whole Way. This comes from old English *holh weg* and refers to 'the road through the hollow', it covers the way to Harlton. Stead Lane takes its name from *stede*, simply meaning 'place, position' and referring to a certain spot on the road, not the destination.

Cracknow Hill means 'crack waggon hill', a reference to how steep it is, thus likely to break any waggon, particularly an overladen one. Edix Hill Hole may be a diminutive for Edward, while there is no doubt the original reference was to the Saxon cemetery here. Fox Hill Down Farm describes the 'hill or valley (ostensibly different aspects of the same thing) by the nook frequented by foxes', Wilsmere Down Farm was originally 'Wulfmaer's down or slope', and Balk Plantation is from *balke* a word denoting 'an unworked ridge separating two cultivated strips'.

Barrington Hall was once home to the Bendyshe family. While the building and spacious grounds date back to the seventeenth century, with later obviously Georgian improvements, the family can trace their family back much further and are one of the oldest in the county.

The local pub here has one of the most common names in the country, indeed the Royal Oak is probably second only to the Red Lion in popularity. It commemorates one of the most famous episodes in English history when, following defeat at the Battle of Worcester in 1651, Charles II and his aide Colonel Carless hid in the Boscobel Oak while the Parliamentarians walked just feet below them during this stage of the pursuit. Years later, at the Restoration of the Monarchy, the king's birthday of 29th May was declared Royal Oak Day.

Bartlow

Records of this name begin with Berkelawe in 1232, which comes from Old English *beorc hlaw* and refers to 'the tumuli where birch trees grow'.

The village skyline is dominated by the ancient burial mounds or tumuli which have given a name to the local pub, the Three Hills. The tallest of these tumuli is held to be the largest in Britain. Looking at the parish church of St Mary's, it is fairly obvious that this is quite unusual for the round tower of the church is quite striking. Whilst not unique, there is a second in the county at Snailwell, there are only 185 in the country of which all but seven are in East Anglia.

Barton

A common place name and usually, as here, the 'barley farm' from Old English *bere tun*. It should also be noted how some places from *bere tun* are a more general reference to 'crops' rather than specifically to 'barley'. The place is recorded as Barton in 1060 and as Bertone in 1086. To a toponymist, one who studies place name origins, this stands out as other Bartons have an addition for distinction.

Here is Whitewell Farm, from *hwit wielle* and meaning 'the fair or clear spring'; Bird's Farm was home to John Birde in 1440; and The Vatches gets its name from its association with Richard de la Vatch, here by 1285.

One pub here is the Hoops, which really does refer to hoops, although maybe not originally to those swung around the waist but those made to hold a barrel together. The White Horse is probably an heraldic reference to the House of Hanover, who ruled in England from the eighteenth century for some 170 years but with only seven monarchs.

Barway

Found in a document dated 1155 as Bergeia, here is a name from Old English *beorg eg* and giving 'the dry ground in marsh with barrows or tumuli'.

Bassingbourn

Domesday's listing of Basingborne differs little to the modern form, however this name is not Norman but Saxon. Here the personal name precedes Old English *inga burna* and describes 'the stream of the family or followers of a man called Bassa'.

Locally we find John O' Gaunts House, named for the market granted by Edward III, firstly to John, Duke of Normandy and later to the man himself, John of Gaunt, the most powerful man in England during the fourteenth century.

Beck Brook

A tributary of the Old West River this name is found as Le Broke in 1483. Despite the French definite article this is not French but from Old Scandinavian *bekkr* and Old English *broc*, which literally speaks of 'the stream brook'.

Benwick

Listed in 1221 as Beymwich, here is the Old English *bean wic* 'the farmstead where beans are grown' or possibly *beam-wic* 'the farmstead of or by the tree trunks'.

Ibberson's Drove was associated with land held by Isaac Ibberson in 1820, while Smith's Farm was associated with the family of Thomas Smith in 1678.

The local is the Five Alls, a name first seen in the seventeenth century and, while there are differences between one pub and the next, shows the public house is open to all who are working together for the common good, both inside and out of this particular establishment. Most often we see a sign where the king states "I rule for all", the parson maintains "I pray for all", the soldier "I fight for all", and the labourer "I work for all".

Benwick stands on an old course of the River Nene on a feature known as a rodham. This term is relevant to the county and used specifically to refer to a topographical feature only seen in the fenlands and normally referred to as a 'roddon' owing to this being used by Major Gordon Fowler, the archaeologist who first wrote extensively about such although it is generally accepted that the correct term is 'rodham'. The origin of this odd feature is disputed for clearly a dried up riverbed would normally be expected to be a hollow or depression, not a raised ridge of land. There are numerous explanations put forward, the most likely being that the riverbed of silt would shrink less as it dried than the surrounding peat lands. This would lead to eventual subsidence of the peat beds and leave the line of silt deposited by the river along its bed standing higher.

Bin Brook

A tributary of the River Cam, this name is found as Le Binnebrok in 1260, Wyttewellebroke in 1349, Cotenbrok in 1437, and Benbrook in 1687. The fourteenth century record is a name which is applied to the upper reaches of this watercourse and tells us it was known as 'the white spring brook'. The present name is from Old English *bionnan broc* and describes 'the land enclosed by a brook'.

Bluntisham

Here is a Saxon personal name followed by the Old English *ham* and speaking of 'Blunt's homestead'. Records of this name survive from 1050 as Bluntesham.

Here the Prince of Wales takes the title of the heir presumptive, while the White Swan may refer to the ubiquitous waterfowl but is more likely an heraldic representation depicting the Vintner's Company.

Bluntisham village sign

Bottisham

Records of this name are found as Bodekesham in 1060 and Bodichessham in 1086. This is a Saxon personal name with Old English *ham* and telling us of 'Boduc's homestead'.

Here Braddons Plantation was planted at 'the broad place'; Bendyshe Farm remembers the family of Thomas de Bendish, known to be here by 1321; St Ives Wood is a reminder of William de Sancto Ivone who was here by 1294; and Allington Hill seems to be taken from William Alyngton, here in 1410, rather than the reverse for there is no record of the place name prior to this. The Bell Inn is the local pub with a name showing the ale house and the church were closely linked.

The east window of the parish church, together with a nearby tablet, are in memory of Colonel Jeyns. This member of the local family was at Balaclava, where the British cavalry rode along the Valley of Death in the face of terrific enemy artillery. The events of the 25th October 1854 were immortalised in Alfred, Lord Tennyson's poem *The Charge of the Light Brigade*. Colonel Jeyns was one of those who survived and returned home.

Bourn

A place name which takes its name from the stream, quite literally for this is Old English *burna* or Old Scandinavian *brunnr* and describing the '(place at) the stream'. This name is recorded as Brune in the Domesday record of 1086.

Barance's Farm remembers Ann Barrans, who was here in 1639; John Gill was associated with Gill's Hill by 1700; Arms Hill gets its name from Alms Hill Farm which, here by 1840, was clearly set aside for the benefit of the poor; and finally the remoteness name of Newzealand, although it is not instantly recognisable as one word.

Pubs here include the Golden Lion, an heraldic sign which can be traced back to Henry I or to the Percy family, dukes of Northumberland. Nobody but Admiral Lord Nelson has more pubs named after him than the Duke of Wellington, whose victory against Napoleon at Waterloo made a national hero of a man who went on to enjoy a successful political career, serving as Prime Minister 1828-30 and Foreign Secretary 1834-35.

Bourn Brook

This is the brook after which the previous place is named and has an identical meaning. This name is found in a document dated 1220 as Brunnebroke.

Bourne, River

A river which feeds the River Granta, the name is recorded as the Burne in 1577 and obviously from Old English *burna* or Old Scandinavian *brunnr* and 'the stream'. However some parts of the river are also known to be recorded as the Withitheburne or 'the withy stream' in 1279, and another stretch is known as Babren in 1586, an example of back-formation from the minor place name of Babraham. These show how any river, simply because of its length and the different kinds of landscape they pass through, will have had a number of different names in the past much more so than they do today. In times when many would have been unlikely to have travelled far from their home, it would probably have been the only river of any size they would ever see and thus they would be unlikely to know the alternative names for 'their' river. Every case must be different but most river names will have become 'fixed' when first noted on a map, thus it would have been pot luck as to what name the cartographer labelled the river with, purely depending upon where he asked the question and of whom. A river has various moods, from its youth as a fast flowing stream in the hills and, as it ages, becoming slower as it meanders across the lowland plains to the sea. As river names are almost always descriptions of the river or what can be seen on and around its banks, clearly the name can differ wildly from person to person.

Boxworth

Domesday lists this name as Bochesuuorde in 1086. Here is 'Bucc's enclosure', with the Saxon personal name followed by Old English *worth*.

Individuals who left their names on the map of Boxworth include William Aspelun, associated with Asplin's Mount in 1279; Bird's Pastures Farm was worked by James Bird by 1763; Page's Farm takes the name of John Page, who was here by 1782; and Samson's Barn was named around 1260, referring either to Geoffrey, son of Sampson, or Matilde Sampson.

The local pub here is the Golden Ball which would seem a candidate for either an heraldic image or perhaps a religious symbol. Yet there is no known connection to any local coat of arms or any theological imagery, so it seems this is nothing more than a simple image. Most pubs of this name also show a cross, this a reference to Constantine the Great, the first Roman emperor to convert to Christianity. However there seems no link to Boxworth.

Brampton

Here are two Old English elements *brom tun* which mean this is 'the farmstead where broom grows' and is recorded as Brantune in 1086.

Street names of Brampton, as elsewhere, tell a history of a place from a unique perspective. Allen's Orchard is a reference to the bricklayer, M. J. Allen, who was born in London and who came here looking for work on the churches around this area. Later his son, who had the same name, served as a parish councillor.

Bernard Road, Olivia Road, and Sparrow Close are named after Brigadier General Robert Bernard Sparrow, who died in 1805 at the age of 32, and his widow Lady Olivia Bernard Sparrow who was a great benefactor for Brampton. Mandeville Road is named after Lord Mandeville, grandson of Lady Olivia Bernard Sparrow.

Local politics is always a favourite for the names of streets, even if it is only Centenary Way which celebrated the centenary of the parish council in 1994. Budge Close is one example, named after Henry Simcoe Budge who came here from his native Cornwall and served as rector from 1882 to 1912 and also as parish councillor for the last ten years. Creot Close remembers Simeon Croot, born in Swineshead in 1860 he served as both surveyor's clerk and also clerk to the parish council from 1894 to his death in 1926. Parish councillor Robert Corrie Evans was the inspiration for Evans Close. Layton Crescent was named after parish councillor Charles Temple Layton. Parish councillors George Lenton and R. J. Lomax gave their names to Lenton Close and Lomax Drive. Charles Laws, who served the community as both parish councillor and funeral director, is remembered by Laws Crescent. Wells Close was named after R. T. G. Wells, who served for many years on the parish council.

Burnaby Close is less clear cut. Emily Burnaby left a donation to set up a charity for the poor in her will of 1893. However there were several other candidates including R. Burnaby, J. C. W. Burnaby. F.G. Burnaby, and H. F. Burnaby, all of whom were members of the clergy.

Carter Close is named after Mr. W. T. Carter who was headmaster of the local school 1932-47. Emery Close is named after a husband and wife team associated with the school, Edward James Emery was headmaster while his wife taught sewing. Flint Close was named after Edward Laundy Flint who was clerk to the School Board. Richard Westbrooke, schoolteacher and long serving Scout Group leader, gave his name to Westbrook Close.

However nobody can have merited a road being named after them for their contribution to education more than Eveline Woolley for whom

Woolley Close was named. She was the wife of former headmaster H. W. Woolley, and had worked in the office there since 1906. In all she spent almost all her life associated with the local school, as first a pupil, then monitress, a teacher, headmaster's wife, headmistress, manager, chairman of the managers, and finally on the Education Committee of the County Council.

Dorling Way remembers Dick Dorling, a Territorial Royal Engineer in the pre-war years, he was captured at Dunkirk and became a prisoner of war held in Poland for the rest of the war. Hilary Lodge is named after Miss Hilary Layton Blunt, who was the leading light for the local Girl Guide movement for many years. Knowles Close is named after Kenneth Davenport Knowles, who was rector in 1912 and went on to become Archdeacon of Huntingdon in 1922.

Horseshoes Way is named after the region where it was cut, the road forming a loop in an area where blacksmiths worked. Miller Way remembers landowner Thomas Miller who died in 1863. Similarly Riddiford Crescent was named after landowner Cecil Riddiford. Page's Way was a fitting tribute to Ernest William Page, who not only worked on the roads during the day for Hunts County Council but recorded much of its history in his spare time as a leading expert on local history. Pepys Road is named after the famous diarist Samuel Pepys who, although he did not live here, visited often.

Brampton was an RAF station and, as such, provided married quarters for those who qualified. These buildings were named after other names associated with the RAF and these have been retained now the region has been developed for civilian use. Hence we find Belle Isle and Belle Isle Crescent from an Irish location; Hansell Road remembers USAF Major General Haywood Shepherd Hansell Jnr; Luqa House will be familiar to those who remember this is now the name of the airport in Malta; North Front House is after the RAF station in Gibraltar; Masirah House is named after the RAF station in Oman; Kyle Crescent remembers Air Marshall Sir Wallace Kyle; Kohima Block was named after the decisive land battle victory over Japan; and Seletar House named after RAF Seletar in Singapore.

Pubs of Brampton include the Black Bull, some pubs of this name may indeed have referred to an impressive favourite animal which was renowned locally, however the vast majority are heraldic and could refer to a number of families. Brampton Mill occupies the site of that former building. The Dragoon Inn is a corruption of 'dragon', a name given to the carbines which were effectively short-barrelled muskets and the name later applied to the soldiers who carried this weapon.

Brington

Listings of this name go back to 974 as Brynintune and as Breninctune in 1086. Here a Saxon personal name is followed by Old English *ing tun* and referring to 'the farmstead associated with a man called Bryni'.

Brinkley

The only record of note here is as Brinkelai in the late seventeenth century, however the name will have existed long before this as it features a Saxon personal name and Old English *leah* and telling us of 'Brynca's woodland clearing'.

Buckden

Here a Saxon personal name is followed by Old English *denu* and describing 'the valley of a woman called Bucge'. The place is found in Domesday as Bugedene.

At Buckden is the Vine, a pub name which was once much more common than it is today. It is also one of the oldest of pub names and would often have been used growing on the sign itself, this would have been purely symbolic for there could never have been enough to produce drink in commercial quantities. This is the original meaning of the name, a reference to wine or vineyards, although the more recent names are probably heraldic and a reference to the Worshipful Company of Distillers.

Buckworth

Recorded in Domesday as Buchesworde, here a Saxon personal name is followed by Old English *worth* and telling us of 'Bucc's enclosure'.

Burrough Green

Seen in 1045 as Burg, in 1086 as Burch, and as Boroughegrene in 1571, this name was originally from Old English *burh* or 'the fortified place' with the later addition of Middle English *grene* or 'the village green'.

Raven's Hall probably took the name of 'raven's wood', although Old English *hrafn* may have been used here as a personal name. Sparrow's Grove does refer to a name, the family of Richard Sparrow were here by 1825. Unfortunately the origin of Plunder Wood is unknown, although it clearly relates to something being taken.

Burwell

From Old English *burh wella* this is 'the spring or stream by the fortified place' and is recorded as Burcwell in 1060 and Buruuella in 1086.

Several minor names recall former inhabitants of Burwell. The street name of Toyse Lane remembers John Toyse, here in 1446; both Baker's Fen and Baker's Drove are named after the family of Thomas Bakere, here by 1394; Bunting's Path remembers Thomas Bunting, here by 1279; and John Dyson was associated with Dyson's Drove some time before 1840. The exception is the remoteness name, that far corner of the parish which was likened to having to walk to the farthest corner of the planet to work, here described as Klondyke Farm.

The Fox is a common pub name, easily recognised, goes well with a multitude of other animals and objects, and is also one of the oldest words for any animal. It can be traced to the forerunner of Old English and to Proto-Germanic *fukhs*, and from there right back to the theoretical mother tongue of Proto-Indo-European and *puk* which is related to Sanskrit *pucca* or 'tail', the fox's most obvious feature.

In what is now named Cuckolds Row, the unfortunate individual who gave this place its name was never recorded, is a plaque marking a tragedy from the eighteenth century. On 8th September 1727 a puppet show arrived to perform to the villagers. Staged in a barn here the available spaces were soon filled and there were still a number of villagers locked outside when the performance started. Clearly barns were unlikely to be fitted with locks and hence it was deemed necessary, in order to prevent unauthorised entry, to nail the barn doors shut. From outside one spectator managed to see something of the performance by peering in through a gap. Unfortunately this gap was also how their lighted candle was knocked into the building where it set fire to the hay therein and started the blaze. As inscribed on the gravestone of St Mary's Church, 78 individuals died in the ensuing fire, of which 51 were children.

Bury

A common place name which is always derived from Old English *burh* and speaking of 'the fortified place, or stronghold'. The name is recorded as Byrig in 974.

This place is the birthplace of bandy, a sport also referred to as Russian Hockey and officially recognised by the International Olympic Committee. Fundamentally this has the same structure as association football in terms of players, playing area and rules, but the players use a hockey stick, a round ball (not a puck) and the game is played on ice. A document from 1813 states that Bury Fen Bandy Club had just achieved the distinction of remaining undefeated for one hundred years. What is not recorded is how many matches were played in this period.

Bythorn

This name comes from Old English *bi thyrne* and describing the '(place) by the thorn bush'. Records of this name include Bitherna in 960 and Bierne in 1086.

C

Caldecote

A name which is recorded as per the modern form in Domesday. This is a common place name, found in various parts of England and always referring to 'the cold or inhospitable cottages' from Old English *cald cot*.

Mitchel's Wood and Stinnage's Wood are reminders of former residents Robert Michel and William Stennet, here by the nineteenth century.

Callow Brook

This tributary of the Beck Brook has few early forms, however the obvious *calu* is highly unlikely for this means 'bald, bare' and is hardly ever seen away from a hill and there is no significant rise in the ground here. Thus it seems this will probably be from 'the brook by Cola's hlaw or mound'.

Cam, River

A name which applies to the river also known as the Granta. Indeed this river may well be able to claim more recorded names along its length than any other in England. As each alternative is, to some degree, still relevant today, each is treated under its own entry. This name is probably the easiest of them all to define, for this is simply taken from the major town, back formation from Cambridge and indeed it is easy to see why it would be thought to refer to 'the bridge over the Cam'. Similarly the river is also known as the Cante which, as can be seen in the following entry, is from the early name for the town of Cantebrigge.

Cambridge

The earliest surviving record of this name is as Grontabricc in 745, with the later 1086 record from Domesday as Cantebrigie. The earlier name is the correct form, referring to 'the bridge on the River Granta', the river name being discussed under its own entry. By the time of the eleventh century the name appears with the Norman pronunciation and eventually affects the name of the river, today known as the Cam by what is known as back-formation.

Cambridge street names include Dolphin Passage, named from the inn here; Drummer Street, derived from *drosn* 'dregs' and *mere* which is understood as 'the dirty pool'; Hobson Street was home to Thomas Hobson, a carrier here by 1630; Jesus Lane is named for the nuns of St Rhadegund, Jesus College later built on the site of the nunnery; Maid's Causeway was where almshouses stood by 1647, specifically for the purpose of just two widows and four maids; Doll's Close is undoubtedly a reference to the same place; Tennis Court Road stands alongside Pembroke College, which is recorded as having a 'tenyse court' in 1564; and Thompson's Lane is a reminder the Thompson family were living here from 1520 until 1750.

Coronation Street was built at the time of the coronation of George IV, the region was formerly known as New Zealand and, for a period afterwards, the postal address continued to be given as: "Coronation Street New Zealand, Cambridge". Similarly an odd postal address was seen when new houses were built on what had been Mill Road, the mill once owned by architect Charles Humphrey (1772-1842). These were the first homes built since the railway came through here, in fact the railway cut right through and the new houses were on the opposite side of the lines. The new buildings were not given a new street name and thus we saw letters addressed to: "--- Terrace, Mill Road Over The Line, Cambridge".

Willow Walk is easily seen as referring to that past the willow trees, an image some may see as their ideal picture of the Garden of Eden. It is this biblical description given to an area where the early theme includes such idyllic names as Orchard Street, Paradise Street, Adam & Eve Street, Prospect Row and Eden Street. Victoria Street is, not unpredictably, named to honour the longest reigning queen in British history. Queen Victoria's name is synonymous with the British Empire, three streets here are lasting reminders of that Empire around the Mediterranean in the names of Suez Road, Cyprus Road and Malta Road.

The tradition of producing rifles, particularly the wooden butt, is seen in the naming of Rifle Butt Row and Rifle Butt Road. In 1859 this road was renamed Ross Street, two years after the founding of the Cambridge Rifle Club. Whilst there is no record of why the road was renamed, it seems impossible this was not because of one E. C. R. Ross who was Champion of All England in 1861 at Wimbledon, when he collected a £250 prize put up by Queen Victoria. However it should be noted the name of the street was not changed until 1888, some 27 years after his valuable win.

Catherine Street is thought to be after a member of the developer's family. A local chemist, who also served one term as mayor, Joseph Sturton gave his name to Sturton Street. The Sturton family came from Sleaford in Lincolnshire, hence the naming of Sleaford Street. Gwydir Street is named after Lord Gwydir, Sir John Wynn (1553-1627). Grafton Street is from John Grafton, the man held to have single-handedly brought gas to the city of Cambridge.

Fitzroy Street is named after Henry Fitzroy, Duke of Grafton the second illegitimate son of Charles II and the Duchess of Cleveland. Burleigh Street recalls local businessman and carrier James Burleigh, while Castle Street is obviously a reference to a fortification. Clearly Magdalen Street comes from the church dedicated to St Mary Magdalen, with St Johns Street near St Johns College Chapel, and All Saints Passage is on land associated with this church.

There are two possible reasons for the naming of Portugal Place, either this was named to mark the Peninsular War or, a more desirable definition in the opinion of the author, would be from port (Portuguese) wine for this was where Portuguese coins were unearthed in the nineteenth century. Both King Street and Malcolm Street were named after King Malcolm IV of Scotland. While a Scottish king may seem an unusual source for a Cambridgeshire street name, he was linked to the county by another title of his, as Earl of Huntingdon.

Green Street takes its name from Oliver Green, former MD of Caius College. Sidney Street occupies land once held by Sidney Sussex College. St Mary's Passage is derived from the nearby St Mary's Church. Similarly Benet Street comes from St Benet's Church, and Little Mary's Lane is from the dedication to St Mary the Less. Free School Lane describes the place of education known as the Perse School.

Rose Crescent was named for the Rose Tavern which once opened its doors to customers here. The name of Petty Cury is a corruption of the French for 'Little Cookery', it is known there were many pastry cooks here at one time and is generally accepted as the basis for this name.

We cannot leave the centre without mentioning the colleges and in this example those who came here to study religion. The clergy of the Cambridge colleges were required to ride out to the villages to take Sunday services. As they would not return until late, Sunday clubs were formed to provide a much needed supper on their arrival. At Kings College the Sunday evening repast always saw the serving of mutton chops, which was why the Sunday club here was known, albeit unofficially, as the Neck or Nothing.

Locally we find Barnwell, either from *beorn wielle* and 'the warrior's spring' or perhaps this is a personal name and 'Beorna's spring'; Butt Green refers to archery butts, used for the obligatory archery practise; Castle End marks the site of the mound of the former Norman castle; from Middle English *coo* comes Coe Fen, the 'fen frequented by jackdaws'; and Empty Common is a misunderstanding of *impe haeg*, meaning 'the sapling enclosure'.

Gravel Hill Farm explains itself as 'the gravelly hill'; similarly Fordfield speaks of 'the river crossing by the open land'; The Hithes refers to that part of the river between two bridges, either a reference to the family who owned this land or maybe it was used as a landing place; the Kings Ditch owes its name to two kings who financed improvements, King John in 1215 and King Henry III in 1267, it marked the eastern limits of the centre; and Merton Hill Farm was left to Merton College, Oxford by Walter de Merton in 1270.

Midsummer Common informs us of a fair held here at this time of year in 1877; from either *niew ham* 'the new homestead' or *niew hamm* 'the new (place) at the hemmed in land' comes the name of Newnham; and Stourbridge Common is from *steor brycg* 'the bridge associated with oxen or cattle'.

Mention Cambridge and many will immediately think of the University Boat Race. This British tradition has led to the naming of a number of pubs in the city, the Boathouse, the Boat Race, and the Champion of the Thames. Other water names here include the Jolly Waterman, Master Mariner, Quay Bar, and Waterside. The Ship is another possible name in this category, however most often it is a corruption of 'sheep'.

Sporting connections with the university are commemorated by the Cambridge Blue, a term telling the individual has represented his university in sporting competition; the Chariots of Fire is named after the events at the 1924 Olympic Games depicted in the film of that name; the Cricketers reminds us the universities have long provided opposition for county sides, not to mention being the proving ground for innumerable players. The Graduate is also university related. The Town and Gown is a phrase which began as a reminder of the divide between the townsfolk and those who came here solely for the universities. The Grasshopper, too, has a university sporting connection for this is name of the lawn tennis club.

Brewing names are perfect for pubs for they advertise the product, it is quite refreshing to find an unusual name in the Tap and Spile, referring to the implements used in tapping the full barrel to draw off the contents.

The Hogshead refers to a large barrel which would hold either ale or perhaps wine, itself the origin of the name of the pub called the Grapes, while the Hopbine remembers the fruit grown to flavour the beer. The Baron of Beef advertises the cut of meat, equal to a double sirloin, which would have been served within.

Symbolism is important in pub names and signs, particularly in days when the majority of the population were illiterate. The Globe suggested everyone was welcome, the Bird in the Hand hopes to convey it was better to have what was on offer here than to aspire for the unattainable, the Seven Stars are those of the constellation known as the Plough and a familiar navigational aid.

Trees were chosen as instantly recognisable, particularly those found nearby. Hence the names of the Chestnut Tree and the Elm Tree. Animals provide a wealth of potential names while also making attractive signs. Here we find the Cow, Eagle, Zebra, Golden Pheasant, the Jenny Wren, and the Pickerel Inn, a pickerel is a young pike. Anglers are attracted by the promise of catching very different fish near the Pike & Eel.

In choosing the name of the local pub the locality is often the best source. The Brook, and its street of Brookfields, are derived from the small stream, the Cambridge Arms and County Arms are self-explanatory, the Castle Inn is in Castle Street, the Kingston Arms in Kingston Street, predictably the Corner House stands at a junction, Fort St George is the name of small island, the Granta the old name of the river, the Grove a minor place name referring to a small wood or copse, the Locomotive and the Tram Depot describe forms of transport, the Maypole would have stood nearby, the Old Spring marks a reliable source of water, and the Mill would have been a well known landmark for many years.

Famous people are always a favourite, especially royalty as in the name of the Alexandra Arms, Queen Alexandra was the consort of Edward VII; the British Queen refers to Boadicea, who famously rebelled against Roman occupation; the Empress can only refer to Queen Victoria, Empress of India while the Jubilee refers to her gold or silver jubilees; the Prince Regent points to the future George III who acted on behalf of his father during what were considered periods of madness; lastly the Royal Standard, the ever evolving emblem of the royal family.

Other individuals and families who gave their names include the Duke of Argyll, husband of Princess Louise, the fourth daughter of Queen Victoria; the Clarendon Arms remembers the earls of Clarendon; the Devonshire Arms after the landowners the dukes of Devonshire; the Earl of Beaconsfield was the title taken by former Prime Minister Benjamin

Disraeli; the Earl of Derby is a title held by the Ferrers family and later created for the Stanleys; the Osborne Arms features a family name traceable back to William Osborn who was in Cambridge by 1310; the Panton Arms recalls the family who were living at Fen Ditton Hall; the Portland Arms recalls the dukes of Portland and included the third duke, William Henry Cavendish Bentinck who was prime minister twice; and the Sir Isaac Newton recalls the physicist and mathematician who is one of our nation's most admired scientists.

More recently, in 1957-58, Sir Vivian Fuchs led the first expedition to traverse the continent of Antarctica. The size of this achievement can be measured by the forty-five year gap between this and the first time the South Pole was reached. Sir Vivian came to Cambridge in 1959 to open the pub which commemorated the event, however it was not named for the man but after the vehicle which enabled them to make the journey, one with caterpillar tracks it is known as the Snowcat.

Historical names here include the Druids, and also the Ancient Druids, members of the Celtic priesthood. While the Alma recalls the battle, an engagement of the Crimean War. Trades gave names to the Bakers Yard, the Carpenters Arms, Wrestlers Arms, and Bun Shop. A name like the Bath House tells us it was on or near the former public baths. Religion is always a favourite subject, both the Five Bells and the Six Bells recall the number of bells in the peal, while the Mitre is named after the hat worn by a bishop.

Heraldic names include the Fleur-de-Lys, representative of France it became a part of the English coat of arms when Edward III assumed the title King of France; the Green Dragon features large on the coat of arms of the earls of Pembroke; the earls of Newcastle are represented by the Greyhound; the image of the Spread Eagle has been adopted by many countries, including the USA, Germany, Russia, Spain, and Roman Empire, with many families also adopting the image; the White Swan is probably used as a pub sign to represent the Vintner's Company, although there are several other more obvious possibilities.

Blackamoors Head is an old name, one which first appeared in the sixteenth century to refer to someone with dark skin. Sir Francis Drake set out to circumnavigate the world on board his ship the *Pelican*, when he returned he had renamed the vessel *Golden Hind* – the name given to the pub – and taken from the coat of arms of Sir Christopher Hatton, Drake's business partner.

Live and Let Live is a pub name where the landlord comments on some trouble which, while he considers them to be unfair, he decides to turn a blind eye and make his comment silently but clearly. The Hat and Feathers is a reminder of the headgear worn by the royalist soldiers most often referred to as Cavaliers. The Fountain Inn may refer to a local spring, or the name may be heraldic and refer to the Plumbers' Company or the Master Mariners. As the patron saint of the nation it is no surprise his most famous conquest stars alongside him outside the George & Dragon.

Among those the local authorities might consider worthy of having a street or square named after them is the cartoonist Ronald Searle. Born in Cambridge in March 1920, his most famous creation are those girls from St Trinian's School, characters now reworked and updated for the film industry of the twenty-first century. Professor Stephen Hawking was Lucasian Professor of Mathematics at Cambridge for over thirty years and still holds a number of important posts despite the medical problems which often overshadow his scientific achievements.

Samuel Pepys was associated with Cambridge for a while, indeed his gratitude for the time spent at university here was acknowledged by him bequeathing his book collection to Magdalene College, where it can still be seen in housed in the building known as the Pepys Building. His will also made clear these should be housed in his original book cases. Amongst the works are naval records including those of the Mary Rose, and the personal almanac of Sir Francis Drake.

For any lover of cricket December 16th 1882 is a momentous day, although nobody truly appreciated this birth for another 23 years. Sir John Berry Hobbs, known to all as 'Jack' and named 'The Master' scored 199 centuries in first class cricket. After making his debut in the second test of the Ashes tour of 1907-8 (he was still suffering from the after effects of sea-sickness for a time and missed the first test) he was always selected until he retired from test cricket in 1930. His 29-year career saw 61 test matches at an average of 56.94, a career aggregate of over 67,000 runs, and is considered the greatest opening batsman the game has ever seen.

Cambridgeshire

The county town with Old English *scir*, an administrative region first mentioned in the eleventh century. Domesday records the name as Grentebrigscire, hence 'the shire of the River Granta'.

Cambridgeshire is home to some of the oldest permanent Neolithic sites in the British Isles, many finds have been uncovered around Isleham. Nearly all counties have nicknames for the inhabitants. Cambridgeshire folk are traditionally known as Cambridgeshire Camels or Cambridgeshire Cranes, taken from the birdlife which inhabits the fens.

Camps (Castle and Shudy)

A name found in Domesday simply as Canpas, the additions are first seen in the thirteenth century as Campecastel and Sudekampes respectively. These additions necessary for these places are little more than a mile apart. Here the basic name comes from the plural of Old English *camp* and referring to 'the field enclosures'. The additions refer to a medieval castle and from Old English *scydd* meaning 'shed, hovel'.

At Castle Camps we find the minor place names of Holmstead Hall and Olmstead Green, both having a common origin in *elm stede* or 'the place of the elm trees'. Willesey tell us it was 'Wifel's enclosure'; John Cooper was at Cooper's Farm by 1840; Hart's House a region associated with the family of John le Hert by 1360; William Park worked Parkin's Farm by 1840; and Little Biggin Common is from Middle English *biggin* or 'building'.

Shudy Camps brings us names like Freckney Pond, the basic name means 'Fraecca's *hoh* or hill spur', this Saxon personal name is a nickname meaning 'greedy, bold' and is probably not intended to be in any way uncomplimentary. Nosterfield End is a difficult name to define, it could be a religious reference and thus an abbreviation of Paternoster, or alternatively this may represent 'the sheep fold field'. Individuals who are remembered in the landscape include William de Berardesheye, who gave his name to Barsey Farm although it may be the family took the existing and unrecorded name of the place meaning 'Beornheard's enclosure'. By 1840 John and Rebecca Carter were working what is now Carter's Farm, while much earlier in 1350 Sir John de Shardelowe was associated with Shardelowe's Farm.

The Cock public house is a fairly common name still, even though the majority point to a former venue for cock fighting which was banned in England from 1835.

Carlton

Listed as Carletunes in 990, Carlentone in 1086, and Carlton in 1260, this name comes from Old Scandinavian *karla* and Old English *tun* and describes 'the farmstead of the freemen or peasants'.

Sir Thomas Elyot is the most famous resident of Carlton. A scholar, diplomat and author he died and was buried here in 1546.

Castor
Derived from Old English *caester*, here is 'the Roman stronghold' which was recorded as Caestre in 948 and as Castre in 1086.

The Prince of Wales Feathers are the three ostrich feathers featured on the symbol of that title, and also outside the pub of that name.

Cat's Water
Another of the county's rivers which has different names, this forms the border with Cambridgeshire and neighbouring Northamptonshire until reaching the Lincolnshire border turning east to become known as the Old South Eau. This name is recorded as Cattesdrit in 1251 and Catteswater in 1315, which would all suggest this is a 'ditch or water channel of a man called Catt'.

Catworth
Listed as Catteswyth in the tenth century and as Catueeorde in Domesday, this name tells us it was 'the enclosure of a man called Catt or Catta', the Saxon personal name followed by Old English *worth*.

One local pub is the Racecourse, a reference to Huntingdon racecourse approximately seven miles east of here. The racecourse was originally at nearby Port Holme, the first race run in 1775, although the next race meeting was not until 1898. Twenty years later it moved to its present location, with improvements from 1953 to 1967 raising it to the importance it holds today. Aside from the steeplechasers, since 1999 September visitors can see the most unusual race held on any racecourse in the land. Here an array of sporting mascots from all forms of sport compete in the coveted Mascot Grand National. Since then it has been won by Beau Brummie Bulldog of Birmingham City FC (1999), Harry the Hornet of Watford FC (2000), Dazzle the Lion of Rushden & Diamonds FC (2001), Chaddy the Owl of Oldham Athletic FC (2002 and 2003), Graham the Gorilla of Finedon Volta FC (2004), Scoop the Squirrel of The Sun newspaper (2005), Mickey the Monkey of the football charity Kick 4 Life (2006), Wacky Macky Bear of Saffron Walden FC (2007 and 2008), and a home victory at last by Stag of Huntingdon Rugby Club (2009).

Caxton

Domesday records this place as Caustone in 1086 and as Kakestune in 1150, this comes from an Old Scandinavian personal name and Old English *tun* and telling of 'Kakkr's farmstead'.

Swansley Wood Farm comes from Old English and describes 'the wood of the peasant'.

The link between pubs and the church has been noted several times in these pages. Sometimes the link is obvious, others are less evident such as the name of the Cross Keys, symbolic of St Peter and also seen in St Peter's Street. Oddly of the two churches here neither are dedicated to St Peter.

The Caxton Gibbet, recorded here since at least the 1670s, still overlooks the village. Those executed here then displayed as a warning to others, the offender would remain until, quite literally, the body fell apart through decomposition. The best known occupant of this gibbet was he who murdered a local man by the name of Partridge. Originally he made good his escape, but made the mistake of returning to the scene of his crime only to boast he had never been apprehended. This proved his undoing and, it is said, he was ordered to by gibbeted alive. If one version is to be believed a local baker soon joined him when he offered bread to the starving man as he hung there. This horrific form of punishment is always referred to as 'English Law', yet there is no official record of this ever being practiced anywhere in England.

Chatteris

Listed as Caeateric in 974 and Cietriz in 1086, here is a Saxon personal name and Old English *ric* telling of 'the raised strip or ridge of land of a man called Ceatta'. However the first element here may be from Celtic *red* or 'wood'.

Locally we find Curtis's Row, home to William Curtis in 1823; in 1812 William Carter and William Cawthorn were associated with Carter's Bridge and Cawthorne's Farm; while much earlier in 1396 Clark's Farm and Robinson's Farm were worked by John Clerk and Richard Robynson respectively.

We also find the Horseway, which is not quite 'the horse road' but could be something similar in being the 'landing place for horses'. However there is also the chance of an alternative *horsc weg* giving us 'the foul or muddy way'. Modern developers like to use themes for their new roads, here birds connected with water are seen in the names of Heronshaw, Kingfisher Close, Gull Way, Tern Gardens, Drake Avenue,

Curlew Avenue, Teal Close, Mallard Close, and Plover Close.

The Cock Inn is probably a simple rural image, although an indication of it being a venue for cock fighting cannot be ruled out entirely. A name such as Honest John does not necessarily refer to someone called 'John', this conveys a character of unquestioned morals and completely trustworthy.

Chatteris claims to be the last refuge of Boudica before her defeat by the Romans. However we do know the first named resident of the town, his story is told in the *Historia Ecclesiastica* by the chronicler Orderic Vitalis. Bricstan of Chatteris was a free tenant who joined the monastery at Ely Cathedral in 1115, to train as a monk but his education was cut short when he was accused of theft and arrested. Imprisoned in London awaiting trial he later told how Saint Etheldreda came to him in a dream and he watched in disbelief as the heavy chains fell away as she drew near. Awaking he discovered this had been no dream for he was fettered no more. When Queen Matilda, wife and consort of Henry I, heard of the miracle she knew this was a man of God and no thief, so she granted him a pardon and he was allowed to go free. There is now a Bricstan room in the church of St Peter and St Paul.

Cheney Water

A tributary of the Cam which takes its name from Cheyney Lodge, the river being listed as Cheyneys broke in 1675.

Cherry Hinton

Here the basic name comes from Old English *hiwan tun* and describes 'the farmstead belonging to a religious community'. The addition is from Middle English *chiri* and describing the many 'cherry trees' which once grew here.

Worth's Causeway was quite deservedly named after William Worts. He died in 1709, leaving £1,500 for the causeway to be constructed between Emmanuel College and the Gogmagog Hills.

One local pub has a name which, while not unique, is one of only three in the land. The Rosemary Branch recalls a time when these were used for decoration, particularly at weddings and funerals representing fidelity and of remembrance. As the church stood nearby perhaps this was chosen to show this public house was used for both wedding breakfasts and wakes.

Another religious link is seen in the name of the Five Bells, the number of bells in the peal. Considering they are named after a group of legendary outlaws, who seem to have had some influence in about half the parishes in a broad band across the middle of England, there are a large number of pubs named after the Merry men, including locally the Robin Hood & Little John. The Unicorn is a mythical beast with a horn said to have magical properties, it was also the name of a Scottish golden coin from the fifteenth century, the word described an arrangement of three horses ahead of a carriage, but as a pub name is probably heraldic and a reference either to Scotland, the Worshipful Company of Wax Chandlers, the Worshipful Company of Goldsmiths, or the Worshipful Company of Apothecaries.

Cherry Hinton Brook
A tributary of the Cam, this is recorded as simply Le Broke in 1511 a name meaning 'the brook'. The present name is an example of back-formation from the previous entry.

Chesterton
One of the easiest place name to define, essentially because it has changed little since the Old English *ceaster tun* and telling us it was 'the farmstead of or by a Roman stonghold'. The name is recorded as Cestretone in 1086.

The local name of Arbury Camp tells us of 'an earthwork'. The Dog & Pheasant a pub name referring to hunting, possibly the organised shoot on the local estate with a gamekeeper although as often the image of the poacher is portrayed. Another quintessential rural image is portrayed on the sign of the Haymakers, a name from the time when much of the community would join in to help, quite literally, making hay while the sun still shines.

Chettisham
The earliest known record is as Chetesham in a document dating from around 1170, which seems to indicate a Saxon personal name and Old English hamm and speaking of 'the hemmed-in area belonging to a man called Ceatt'. However, as with Chatters, the first element may be an old Celtic *red* meaning 'wood'.

Cheveley

Recorded as Chauelai in 1086 and as Ceafle in 1200, this name comes from Old English *ceaf leah* and describes 'the wood full of fallen twigs'.

The name of Banstead Manor remembers former resident John de Benstede, here in 1315, while Castle Plantation was named for its location next to the old castle ditch.

Childerley

A name recorded as Cildrelai in 1086, Childerl in 1267, Chyldereley in 1272, and Chelderle in 1439. This is Old English *cild leah* and refers to 'the woodland clearing of the young men'.

Chippenham

From a Saxon personal name and Old English *hamm*, this is 'the river meadow of a man called Cippa'. The name is recorded as Chipeham in 1086.

Minor names here include Badlingham, in early Saxon times a separate settlement known as 'the homestead of the people of Baeddel'. Sounds Farm is a misheard pronunciation of 'sands', while Richard Giffard was associated with Gifford Wood by 1238. Jerusalem Wood occupies land belonging to the Domo Hospitalis Jerusalem in 1204, hence the name, with the French sounding La Hogue Hall was built by Edward Russell who commanded the English fleet which defeated the French at La Hogue in 1692 and named the hall to mark the victory.

Originally called the Hope Inn, the village pub changed its name in the late nineteenth century. The Tharp family came to Chippenham in 1792, when John Tharp purchased the estate from his inheritance, a result of his great-great-grandfather being one of the original settlers and plantation owners in Jamaica. While the sign predictably depicts the coat of arms of this family, it does also feature an image of the mysterious Tharp Lady. Her stone image looms above the gateway to Chippenham Hall, which has played host to a long list of members of the aristocracy over the years, including royalty. Legend has it on New Year's Eve on the stroke of midnight the stone lady comes to life and descends from her lofty perch to dance on the old driveway.

Chishill (Great and Little)

Recorded in Domeday as Cishella, this comes from Old English *cis hyll* and describes this as 'the gravelly hill'. The additions are self-explanatory and required for two places separated by less than a mile.

Coates

The earliest listing is as Cotes in 1280, the name coming from Old English *cot* and referring to 'the cottages, the huts'. The village is known is famous for its petanque competition which attracts interest from all around Europe.

Coldham

This name has not changed at all since it first appeared in 1251. This comes from Old English *cald hamm* and refers to 'the exposed hemmed in land'.

Colne

A name seen in Domesday exactly as today, this is a lost river name, a Celtic name of uncertain meaning.

The local pub is the Green Man, a name depicted by sign painters in several ways, although all come from the woodsmen or foresters modern signs often show a Robin Hood figure.

Comberton

Here is a Saxon personal name with Old English *tun*, a name recorded in Domesday as Cumbertone and referring to 'the farmstead of a man called Cumbra'.

Swayne's Lane was home to the family of Walter Sweyn by 1279, while The Offal is a rather uncomplimentary evolution from 'the old *feld* or open land'.

Two pubs here advertise two different traditional aspects of the public house, the Grapevine refers of course to the product, while the other arm of the trade is the blacksmith represented here by the Three Horseshoes, which may seem an unusual name until we realise it is a question.

Conington

This place near St Ives is recorded as Cunictune in the tenth century and as Coninctune in Domesday. Derived from Old Scandinavian *konungr* and Old English *tun*, this is 'the king's manor or estate'.

The parish church of St Mary has a noticeably lopsided spire.

Conington

The second place of this name in Cambridge, this version is near Sawtry and has identical origins with the previous entry. However here the tenth century record in Cunningtune and the Domesday entry is Cunitone.

The name of the White Swan public house is normally heraldic, found in many coats of arms including the Vintners' Company, Poulters' Company, Musicians' Company, earls of Essex, Edward III, although of course it may simply be the waterfowl.

Coppingford

Domesday records the name as Copemaneforde, a name meaning 'the ford used by merchants' and clearly one leading to a regular market. The name is a hybrid of Old Scandinavian *kaul mathr* and Old English *ford*.

Coton

A common place name, which nearly always comes from the plural of Old English *cot* and meaning 'cottages, huts'. It is recorded in Domesday as Cotis.

Catherine Hall Farm was a possession of St Catharine's College by 1476. The local reflects the rural location, the Plough being a common pub name.

Cottenham

Found in 948 as Cotenham and as Coteham in 1086, here is a name from a Saxon personal name and Old English *ham* and referring to 'Cotta's homestead'.

Twenty Pence Road ran alongside a place known for its 'twenty pens or folds' in 1596. Alboro Close is from *ald burh* or 'the old fortification'. Chear Fenn comes from Old English *cear*, meaning literally 'turn' and describing this twisting way through the fenland. The Lots tells us this was an allocation of land, one of several areas shared amongst a number of locals.

Setchel Fen was known as 'the enclosure where sedge grows; Smithey Fen tells of the 'smooth, low-lying land'; while early records of Top Moor show this was known as 'Taeppa's marsh'. Individuals who are remembered in the landscape include Jabez Ablett, after whom Ablett's Row is named, Edward Mason gave his name to Mason's Pastures both here in 1840, William Taylor was associated with Taylor's Lodge in 1780, and Lamb's Cross home to Henry Lamb in 1279.

Time and again in the fenlands of Cambridgeshire we find the field name of the Undertakers. This is not, as we might think, a sign of a burial ground or those who made their living by disposing of corpses. This always refers to fenland which has been drained, the very name tells us those who undertook to dig the drains and ditches did so on the basis they would receive a share of the reclaimed land in return, thereafter turning to farming. Of course the Undertakers were far more numerous than the Adventurers, a name also seen around reclaimed land for they too received land in return for investing money supporting the Undertakers while they were working.

The Hop Bind is a pub name which is derived from the hop, the fruit which is used in brewing. The name is not quite correct, for the true description is a hop bine where the plant grows in a helix around a supporting frame or another plant. The Jolly Millers suggests an association with those in the trade and would be particularly content to be there, the addition of 'Jolly' being a common invitation. The Waggon and Horses reminds us of the only way of transporting large quantities of goods until the building of the canals, public houses often acting as agents and distributors.

The local church has a strange narrative told regarding its construction. It made sense to build the church as close to the centre of the community as possible, collectively this makes everyone's journey as short as possible. The church of All Saints had stood at one point of the village and, when it was agreed to move it, began to remove the blocks of stone and transport them to the new site. However next morning it was discovered every stone had been returned to the original site. On hearing the news the parishioners were so troubled they decided it would be better to leave their church where it stood.

Coveney

Two potential origins for this name, the record of Coueneia in 1060 favours neither definition. If this is Old English *cofa eg* then this is 'cove island', or the first element may be a personal name in which case this is 'Cofa's island'.

Minor names here include Wardy Hill, from *weard eg* this means 'the watch-out island'; Barber's Drove recalls the family of Elizabeth Barber, who were certainly here by 1650; and Jerusalem is not a religious name as such, it is on the parish boundary and suggests this part of their domain was far flung, this being an example of what is known as a 'remoteness' name.

Covington

Recorded in Domesday as Covintune in 1086, this name is from a Saxon personal name and Old English *ing tun* and telling us of 'the farmstead associated with a man called Cofa'.

Cranbrook Drain

Listed as Cranebrooke by the Westwater in 1659 and Crainbrook in 1700, this is a boundary stream between the parishes of Sutton Fen and Earith Fen. The most likely origin for this name is seen where this watercourse passes through Willingham, a minor name of Crane's Fen is mistakenly thought to feature a personal name when the real origin of both the place and this stream is 'the brook frequented by cranes or herons'.

Croxton

Two potential origins for this name, the record as Crochestone in 1086 does not adequately clarify the name. Either this is Old English *croc ton* and describes 'the farmstead of a nook of land', or the alternative Old Scandinavian personal name for the first element gives 'Krokr's farmstead'.

Two spinneys are named after former residents of Croxton in 1689: Ingles Spinney remembers the family of William Ingree, while the family represented by Richard Kynge were associated with King's Spinney.

Croydon

Listed as Crauuedene in Domesday, this name comes from Old English *crawe denu* and speaks of this being 'the valley frequented by crows'.

Local names of note include Clopton, from *cloppa tun* or 'the farmstead of the hills'; in 1198 Rouses Wood was home to a man recorded as both Simon Ruffus and Simon Rus; and Gilrags Wood was recorded as Jilrags Wood in 1840, a name which seems certain to have been derogatory 'Jill rags'.

D

Darcey Lode

Normally when defining place names it helps to find as many early forms as possible, while an idea of how the name has developed can often help immensely. However here there are so many records, all they do is show how the name has been confused almost since it was first created. Historical records include Darsey in 1437, Dazzie in 1589, Derseyloade in 1612, Darcy Ea in 1616, Darsey Eye in 1617, while earlier we find Dollode, Dawe Load, and Dar Load and many others which cannot be taken as evidence for they are so different they may not even refer to the same watercourse.

There are two quite different possible sources for this name, either a reference to the river itself or maybe taken from a neighbouring field somewhere along its course. In the first instance there are two equally plausible Old English origins, either this is *deores ea* and 'the animals stream' or perhaps indirectly referring to the stream as 'the stream of the wild animal ford' from *deorfordes ea.*

The alternative is an Old Scandinavian and Old English hybrid in *daevin land* which describes 'the muddy land' or perhaps the first element is related to Icelandic *dafla*, when this then becomes the 'land where it is possible to dabble or splash'. It does seem unlikely this name will ever be fully understood.

Deeping Gate

The earliest surviving record of this name is as Depynggate in 1390, a name featuring the Old Scandinavian *gata* and describing 'the road to Deeping'. Deeping is a place, or more accurately four places, in neighbouring Lincolnshire and all are derived from an Old English *deoping* telling of 'the deep or low-lying place'.

Delph, River

A name not recorded until 1821, when it is found as the Delph or Thirty Feet. The earlier record of 1617 as Delph may be coincidental and not refer to this particular channel, itself dug to help make the Washlands less appropriately named. Draining into the Ouse this is derived from Old English *gedelf* which is most often used for a 'quarry' but should really be understood as 'digging' which is how it is used here.

Denton

Found as Dentun in the tenth century and as Dentone in the Domesday record of 1086, this name is found across England and, as here, is usually from Old English *denu tun* or 'the farmstead in a valley'.

Devil's Dyke, The

A Saxon earthwork where the last phase of construction has been dated to the late sixth and early seventh centuries. This is the largest of any major ditch in the county, built to provide a barrier between tribes, it also crossed the Icknield Way and may have enabled them to control trade in this way. This is now a scheduled monument, a public footpath runs its entire length and provides a chalk grassland habitat with a number of rare species of flora.

Of course a name such as this cannot have failed to attract a number of stories. One has no direct mention of the Devil himself, but features a Saxon chieftain called Rothgar and his beautiful daughter Haenna. The land was tormented by a number of demons, the most feared of which was the Fire Demon who approached Rothgar one day saying he desired his daughter and would have her. Her father told Haenna not to fear, for he had a friend in the Water God who would protect them.

When Rothgar heard the fire demon had a new ally in the Tempest God, the chieftain went to the giants of the forest and told them of his plans. Thus together they started constructing the great ditch, the work continuing for three whole days. As they worked the Tempest God sent a great storm of wind, then hail, and lastly snow. However the work continued in spite of the terrible conditions.

The storm of the Tempest God died down and the men continued until a cloud of smoke with the sound of crackling and spitting heralded a fire approaching along the ditch. Rothgar called out not to fear the Fire Demon, that the Water God would protect them. However, one by one as the fire closed in the giants fled but Rothgar carried on working. Eventually he broke through and the waters of the Cam flooded the ditch, putting the fire out and there was great cheering now both they and Haenna were safe.

The people came to the ditch, dropping offerings into the water as thanks to the Water God. The Fire Demon was not seen again, however a large black dog has been reported roaming along the dyke. A fearsome beast with large blood red eyes, he keeps an eye on the Devil's Dyke and perhaps also protects the treasure said to be buried beneath it.

Diddington

Domesday's record of Dodinctun shows this to come from a Saxon personal name and Old English *ing tun* and meaning it was 'the farmstead associated with a man called Dodda or Dudda'.

Doddington

Recorded as Dundingtune around 975 and as Dodinton in Domesday, this name features a Saxon personal name followed by Old English *ing tun* and tells us it was 'the farmstead associated with a man called Dudda or Dodda'.

The local name of Copalder has been misunderstood, for it was originally *kex alder* 'the dry hollow stem alder' and has been changed to *coppede alder* or 'the pollarded alder'. Ransom Moor began as 'the projecting land where ravens are seen'; Barrot's Farm was home to Henry Barrett in 1529; Lambe's Plantation was associated with Richard Lamb in 1678; Loom's Farm was named after the family of Edward Loomes, here by 1802; and Thicken's Farm remembers Bowen Thickens, a gentleman with a wondrous name who was certainly here some time before 1819.

The pub here is the Three Tuns, this tun being a large cask holding 252 gallons of wine or beer, such vast containers used solely for distribution. Here there are three such containers, showing this is a reference to the Worshipful Company of Vintners and also the Worshipful Company of Brewers.

Downham

From Old English *dun ham* and meaning 'the homestead on or by a hill', this name is recorded in Domesday as Duneham.

Dry Drayton

Drayton is one of the most common place names in the country, indeed the addition here is to distinguish it from Fen Drayton. This comes from Old English *draeg tun* and describes either 'the farmstead near a portage or slope used for dragging down loads' or 'farmstead where drays or sledges are used'. When dragging a load it helps if the ground is wet and yet the addition says this was clearly 'Dry' and hence the second definition is the more likely. However dry does not necessarily mean 'arid', indeed the fenland around the county would make this improbable and thus we should understand this as being 'dryer', that is not always wet depending upon the season.

Two remoteness names here are linked, for that part at the extreme north of the parish is known as Edinburgh Farm which is north of Scotland Farm.

The Black Horse is a pub name which is undoubtedly heraldic, although just what it represents is almost always impossible to say. Aside from being symbolic of a well known bank, it is also used by the goldsmiths, is the nickname of the 7th Dragoon Guards and is a part of innumerable family coat of arms.

Dullingham

Recorded as the modern form in 1045, although by the time of Domesday in 1086 this had become Dullingeham. Here is a Saxon personal name with Old English *inga ham* and referring to 'the homestead of the followers of a man called Dulla'.

Bedham Hill gets its name from Old English *bydel hlinc* or 'the hill by a hollow', while by 1395 John Heylok was associated with Harlock's Moor.

Duxford

Listings of this name include Dukeswrthe in 950 and Dochesuuorde in 1086, which features Old English *worth* preceded by a Saxon personal name and telling of 'Ducc's enclosure'.

Local names describe 'the bare hill' from *calu dun* and today seen as Cloderton. The same Old English language gave us 'the exposed hemmed in land', from *cald hamms* easily recognised in the modern name of Coldhams. Crackwell Hole, a place name telling us it was 'the stream banks overgrown with brushwood'. Pepperton Hill was once the site of 'Pipere's tun or farmstead'. Temple Farm is a common indication that, as here, the Knights Templar held this manor, records showing they were here by 1275. Slow Line is a corruption of *slah* and refers to 'the lane where sloes (juniper berries) are found'. Individuals who have left their mark on the map of Duxford in its minor names include Anthony Barker and Henry de Lacy, who were associated with Barkers Farm in 1550 and Lacey's Farm in 1279, respectively.

The pubs of Duxford include the John Barleycorn, not a person but jocular terminology for a beer or ale. Hardly, if ever, used today, 'he' is the subject of a folksong which humorously suggests that drink is the best friend of all and which says:

Though the Hawthorn the pride of our hedges may be,
And the rose our gardens adorn,
Yet the flower that's sweetest and fairest to me,
Is the bearded Barleycorn.
Then hey for the Barleycorn,
The Bonny Barleycorn,
No grain or flower
Has half the power
Of the Bearded Barleycorn.
Tho' the purple juice of the grape ne'er find
Its way to the cup of horn,
'Tis little I care—for the draught to my mind,
Is the blood of the Barleycorn.
Then hey for the Barleycorn,
The Bonny Barleycorn,
No grain or flower
Has half the power
Of the Bearded Barleycorn.
Tho' the Justice, the Parson and eke the Squire,
May flout us and hold us in scorn,
Our staunch boon friend, the best Knight in the shire,
Is stout Sir John Barleycorn.
Then hey for John Barleycorn,
The merry John Barleycorn,
Search round and about,
What Knight's so stout
As bold Sir John Barleycorn?

The name is also seen in the writings of Robert Burns, Sir Walter Scott and Nathaniel Hawthorne, although not always seen in the same light but always referring to the demon drink.

E

Earith

The earliest surviving record of this name is as Herheth in 1244, a name which comes from Old English *ear hyth* and describes 'the muddy or gravelly place'.

Earith Sign

Two years after cessation of the hostilities in the Second World War, the Battle of Earith Gap was fought on 17th March 1947. However no bullets were fired here. High tides and melting snow tore a fifty yard gap in the river bank, allowing the waters to flow unabated for five days across the fens. Eventually the breach was stemmed by amphibious vehicles until a more permanent solution could be found.

Eastern Brook

A tributary of the Bourne Brook which flows to the east of Eltisley village. The area here is recorded as Estenddene in 1500 and Easton Field in 1840, thus the river name is taken from *east denu* 'the eastern valley'.

Easton

One of the most common place names in the land it is also one of the most simple. Listed as Estone in Domesday, this comes from Old English *east tun* and describes 'the eastern farmstead'. The name also tells us that it was referred to as such by a settlement to the west, although we will never know which.

Eastrea

Listed as Estereie in 1020, this name comes from Old English *eastor eg* or 'the eastern part of the island' - the island in question being Whittesey.

The local pub is the Nags Head, when a nag was a short stocky horse or pony which was available to hire. Today the term 'nag' is used to describe a horse without any pedigree or of poor quality. It is also used to refer to a woman who constantly complains, particularly to her husband. However the ladies should also note this is a comparatively modern development, for a long time the human 'nag' was applied strictly to males!

Eaton Socon

Recorded in Domesday as Etone, this was originally Old English *ea tun* of 'the farmstead by the river'. The addition is Old English *socn*, telling us it was 'the district with right of jurisdiction'.

Local names include Basmead Manor, a place owned by the Bathonia (or Bath) family during the reign of King John at the beginning of the thirteenth century, the suffix has no etymological value it is simply influenced by neighbouring Bushmead. The name of Bushmead is another corruption meaning 'bishop's meadow', although this has no religious connection but is a family name. Little is known of the Bishop family, however we do have a record of a Hugh Bisshope, who was accused of trespassing in Eaton and Cadbury, showing the family were here by the thirteenth century.

Beggary comes from Middle English *beggere* 'beggar' and *baronie* 'the domain of the baron', together referring to 'the domain of the beggar'. Duloe is thought to come from Old English *dyfel hoh*, a reference to its shape as 'the peg-shaped spur of land'. Eatonford Farm is a transferred name meaning 'the ford of Eaton'. Garden Wood is listed as Gardynesgrave, however this seems to refer to 'garden of the grove' which makes no sense. Thus this must be from Middle English *gardeyn* and thus 'guardian of the grove'.

Goodwick features a female Saxon personal name and Old English *wic*, telling us of 'Godgifu's dairy farm'. From *hunig denu* comes Honeydon, the name describing 'the valley where honey is plentiful'. From *stapol hoh* or 'the hill marked by posts' we find the modern name of Staploe, while 'Wigbeald's tun or farmstead' is today seen as Wyboston.

A local pub is the Bell, a simple image which shows the long association between pub and church. While this seems a strange liaison today, during the days when the community worked the land these were the only two places where most would meet. Many pubs use prominent trees as names for they are long-lived and stand out in the landscape, hence the name of the Eaton Oak; the George & Dragon refers to the nation's patron saint and his most famous exploit; the Old Sun also features a simple image, while also suggesting a warm welcome; the Waggon and Horses shows how pubs would act as distribution points before the coming of the canals and later railways; the Wheatsheaf is heraldic, referring to both the Worshipful Company of Bakers and the Brewers' Company; the White Horse Inn symbolises the royal House of Hanover; the Highwayman may well have housed those once feared by travellers, however it should be remembered these rogues were later seen in a more romantic light and this image would have been utilised by landlords.

Ellington

Recorded as Elintune in 1086, this name is either Old English *ael ing tuan* 'the farmstead associated with catching eels' or the first element is a Saxon personal name and thus 'the farmstead associated with Ella or Eli'.

Locals enjoy a glass of their favourite tipple in the Mermaid, which is probably heraldic and a clear reference to the sea, possibly even the famous statue at the entrance to the harbour at Copenhagen.

Elm

Predictably this is the '(place at) the elm trees'. Found as Elm and Eolum in tenth century records, the Old English word was also *elm* and is one of the oldest unchanged words in the English language.

Minor names of this place include Beauford House, itself from an old place name derived from *beaw* describing 'the ford infested by gadflies'. Coldham tells us it was 'the exposed water meadow'; Crowmere began as *crumb dic* telling us of 'the winding ditch'; Friday Bridge was where monks fished for the traditional Friday fare; Halfpenny Field stands alongside a dike, the field name telling the levy attached for the maintenance of that flood barrier; Laddus Fens points to 'the fen by the weir'; Livermere speaks of this as 'the dark muddy pool'; Waldersea was once 'Wealdhere's *eg* or dry land in a marsh'; Boyce's Bridge was associated with John Boyce by 1482; while earlier John Stegge was living at Stag's Holt in 1327.

The public house named after a pickpocket may not seem particularly inviting. However the character is the Artful Dodger, a lovable rogue who befriends the eponymous character in Charles Dickens' novel Oliver Twist; at the Blacksmiths Arms the name shows the village metalworker would work hand in hand with an inn-keeper to their mutual benefit; and the Sportsman began life as an advertisement of a number of games being played here.

Elsworth

Recorded as Eleswurth in 974 and as Elesuuorde in 1086, this name comes from a Saxon personal name and Old English *worth* which tells us this was 'the enclosure of a man called Elli'.

It comes as no surprise to find Coldwell End referring to 'the cold spring'; John Brown was working Brown's Farm by 1290; while Rogue's Lane Farm, and indeed Rogue's Lane, probably refer to 'rascally fellows' rather than terribly evil and dangerous individuals.

Locals enjoy a drink at the Poacher, an image of the lovable rogue who many would turn a blind eye to for their larder could also benefit from his activities.

Eltisley

Domesday records this name as Hecteslei, while by 1228 the name is seen as Eltesle. This is undoubtedly Old English *leah* preceded by a personal name and 'the woodland clearing of a man called Elti'.

Papley Grove is a name which today refers to a small wood or grove, however the name tells us it was once applied to the larger 'woodland clearing of a man called Pappa'. The Leeds Arms remembers the family who were lords of this manor from the late eighteenth century.

Elton

Old records of this name are found as Aethelingtun in the tenth century and as Adelintune in Domesday. This name comes from Old English *aetheling tun* or 'the farmstead of the princes' or the first element is a personal name followed by *ing tun* and is 'the farmstead associated with a man called Aethel'.

The Black Horse is a common element in heraldry, used by a high street bank, goldsmiths, and the 7th Dragoon Guards, amongst many others. Indeed it has been the choice of so many families it is impossible to recognise which family it commemorates.

Ely

From Old English *ael ge* this place name is one of the few which is still referred to by its original meaning as 'the island where eels are to be found'. The name is recorded as Elge in 731 and as Elyg in 1086, the 'island' is simply dry ground in what was once extensive marshland.

Street names here remember Richard Kilby in Kilby's Corner, John Mepsale at Mepsale's Corner, and Radulphi Smale near Smale's Corner, who were all in residence by 1418 and probably knew one another quite well. Smockmill Alley tells us this would have been marked by its windmill, for a smock is a windmill with a revolving top.

Ely St Mary, named after the church, has a St Mary's Street and an Egremont Street which remembers Thomas de Akerman who was living here in the fourteenth century. What became Turbutsey Farm was formerly an independent Saxon settlement known as 'Tidbeorht's *eg* or dry land in marsh'.

Pubs here include the Minster Tavern, which stands with the shadow of the largest building in the city. Other buildings here gave names to the Town House and the West End House, both describing their location. Transport links the names of the Cutter Inn and the Flyer Hotel, the former is the vessel once popular with excise men when on the hunt for smugglers, while the latter was never airborne but the name of a famous stagecoach. The Fountain may have a link to the sea as a symbol representing the Master Mariners, yet is also found on the badge of the Plumbers' Company.

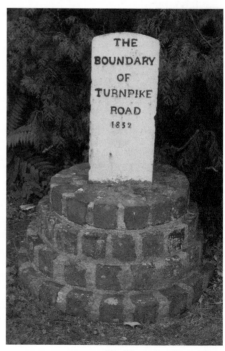

Ely Turnpike Boundary

Royalty is a popular theme with innkeepers, the Kings Arms is one heraldic version, the Royal Standard a more general appreciation of the ever-changing images which trace the course of English history through symbolism and can be read like the pages of a book, should you know the

Ely Cathedral

language. Of course the monarch most associated with Ely is Hereward the Wake, whose stand against the all-conquering Normans lasted longer than any. No surprise to find the name in a local pub called simply the Hereward.

May 1816 and unrest throughout the country erupted locally as the Ely and Littleport Riots. Following the economic drain of the Napoleonic Wars, unemployment and rising grain costs emphasised the gulf between the wealthy and the rest of the population. With little else to do the drink fuelled masses turned on the more affluent quarters, hurling projectiles at the houses and insults at their occupants.

All local attempts to quell the troubles were inadequate, hence Lord Liverpool's government sent in troops who rounded up some 82 people. Edward Christian, brother of Fletcher Christian of the famous Mutiny aboard the Bounty, had been appointed Chief Justice in 1800 and, together with a hastily assembled commission, tried those arrested in the week commencing 17th June 1816. In all 23 men and one woman were condemned, although later the woman and nine men had their sentences commuted to twelve months imprisonment, nine men were commuted to penal transportation ranging from seven years to life, with the remaining five hanged on the 28th of that month.

Russian Canon, Ely

Ermine Street

This Roman road from London to Lincolnshire passes through Cambridgeshire. A name derived from Old English *inga straet* following a Saxon personal name. We can be certain this name was derived from one small stretch of the route, near Arrington and a place name of identical origins. It is no surprise to find a long road named after one small stretch, Watling Street is another example and the definition of many river names simply cannot refer to most of the watercourse.

This name was later transferred to another Roman road near Gloucester, it must have been deliberate as there can have been no confusion here. One theory suggests these names were so well known they were given to other Roman roads for they suggested a sense of security. Even during the reign of William the Conqueror this was one of four roads afforded special policing, heavy penalties being imposed on those who were found to be breaking the King's laws.

Etton

Listed in the early twelfth century as Ettona, this name features a Saxon personal name followed by Old English *tun* and describing 'Eata's farmstead'.

Eversden (Great and Little)

Two places which are less than a quarter of a mile apart and share a common origin. However the records of Euresdone in 1086, with the later Everesdon Magna and Eversdon Parva in 1240, mean we are unable to tell if this is Old English *eofor dun* 'the hill of the wild boar' or if the first element is a personal name and thus 'Eofor's hill'. The additions seen in the thirteenth century are simply Latin *magna* and *parva* for 'great' and 'little' respectively.

Holbein Farm is named after its former owner, John Holben having worked this land from at least 1811.

Eye

This name is first found in the tenth century as Ege, which is closer to the original Old English *eg*. Here is a name which literally means 'the island' and is understood as referring to the 'dry land in the marsh'.

The local is the Red Lion, the most common pub name in the land and one of heraldic origins. It has two possible meanings, most refer to Scotland although it could also point to John O' Gaunt, the most powerful man in England during the fourteenth century. The Spade and Shovel does not really have any etymological story behind it, but for a pub name it is

Eye village sign

ideal for it features two easily recognised images and also the advertisers joy, aliteration.

Eynesbury

Recorded as Eanulfesbyrig at the end of the tenth century and as Einuluesberie in Domesday, here is a Saxon personal name with Old English *burh* and meaning 'the stronghold of a man called Eanwulf'.

The local is the Cambridgeshire Hunter, a name which harks back to the days when public houses would have been meeting places for the hunt.

F

Farcet

Found as Faresheued in the tenth century, here is a name from Old English *fearr heafod* and referring to 'the headland of the bulls'.

As a pub name the Black Swan is heraldic, used since Roman times as a rara avis 'a rare bird' to refer to something or someone rare or unique. Until the discovery of Australia and its indigenous species of black swan it was thought that every swan was white. Another rare creature is the Great Crested Newt, Britain's largest species of newt, which has an area marked out here and dedicated to ensuring its continued existence.

Fen Ditton

This name is recorded as Dictunae in 975, a common place name from Old English *dic tun* or 'the farmstead by a ditch or dyke'. The addition is first seen in 1286 as Den Dytton and comes from Old English *fenn* or 'marshland'.

Biggin Abbey has two elements, the first speaks of this as a 'building, dwelling place', however the second is unknown as it certainly has no connection with an abbey or any other religious order. However the second element of Wadloes Footpath is easily recognised as it is a modern addition to what was known as 'the hill where wheat grows' by the Saxons.

Pubs here include the Kings Head, a name which clearly shows support for the crown rather than one specific monarch. The Blue Lion is more specific, an heraldic representation of the Danish royal family, connected to Britain through Queen Anne, consort of James I. The Ancient Shepherds is a pub name which clearly shows an allegiance to the wool trade, however the addition of 'Ancient' is not a true indication of great age but added to give the name apparent greater dignity.

The Bumps is an annual race rowed on the river where the boats race in single file and attempt to catch and 'bump' the boat in front. This rarely results in actual contact, indeed in the modern era simply passing the stern of the boat in front is considered a 'bump'. Clearly, unlike the normal racing idea, this takes up much less room and thus opens narrower waterways as viable courses.

Fen Drayton

A name which is found as Draegtun in 1012, as Draitone in 1086, and as Fendreiton in 1188. Here is a common name, hence the addition, from Old English *draeg tun* and describing 'the farmstead where drays or sledges are used'. Such would have been useful here for the second part of the name tells us it was a fenn or 'marshland', where a wheel would be a hindrance.

Honey Hill was named for the sticky and glutinous mud to be found at the base of the slope; Daintree's Farm is named after Thomas Daintree, here in 1637; and Middleton's Farm remembers William Middleton, here by 1749.

Fenstanton

With records of Stantun in 1012, as Stantone in 1086, and as Fernstanton in 1260, this name is easy to see as being derived from Old English *fenn stan tun* and describe 'the farmstead on stony ground within an area of marshland'.

The local is the King William IV, the third son of George III who earned the nickname of the Sailor King. He joined the Royal Navy as a midshipman in 1779, soon rising to the rank of captain. However his reluctance to follow orders combined with general indiscipline meant he never commanded a ship, and was as unpopular as an admiral as he was as a monarch.

The village lies on the Roman road named the Via Devana, the route between Cambridge and Godmanchester. The Roman stronghold was established here following an attack on the IX Legion Hispana as they were retreating from Boudica's forces who lain in wait to ambush them at Cambridge.

Fenton

A name found in other counties too, this example being recorded as Fentun in 1236. All these places come from Old English *fenn tun* and refer to 'the farmstead in marshland'.

Fleam Dyke

The earliest records of this name are simply as The Ditch, later Balsham Ditch, and also High Ditch. The modern name comes from Old English *flemena* or 'fugitives', thought to be a reference to this being a defensive feature associated with the last stand of the East Anglians, fleeing ahead of the advancing Roman forces. However evidence, in the form of late Bronze Age pottery shows this is much older, at least at its eastern end.

Today a pathway runs the entire length of the dyke and is a Scheduled Monument, maintained by English Heritage. When planning to walk these four miles the author read how he should look out for the rare Common Juniper tree. This seeming contradiction is, of course, due to Common Juniper being the name of the species.

Fletton

Actually two places, Fletton and Old Fletton, although it is difficult to tell where one ends and the other begins today, even on a map. The name is found as Fletun in Domesday, this comes from Old English *fleot tun* and describes 'the farmstead on a stream'. Normally the term *fleot* is seen as 'tidal stream', however here that is simply not possible for this is more than twenty miles from the coast and it is difficult to see how this can be the case here.

Folksworth

Domesday lists this name as Folchesworde, featuring a Saxon personal name and Old English *worth* and referring to 'Folc's enclosure'.

Fordham

Listed as Fordham in the tenth century and as Fordeham in Domesday, this name comes from Old English and is either *ford hamm* 'the ford by the hemmed in place' or ford ham and 'the ford by a homestead'.

The name of Carter Street is a reminder that this was the home of John Carter in 1567. The Crown Inn is a common pub name showing support for the monarch, indeed it would undoubtedly be the most common in the land were it not that a significant proportion have a second element for distinctiveness. An unusual name, the White Pheasant strictly speaking is not actually 'white' but features the outline of the most colourful game bird on a white background and was probably originally chosen as such was on the menu.

Fowlmere

A name found in 1086 as Feuglemaere, this telling of 'the lake frequented by birds' and derived from Old English *fugol mere*. There is a feature here called the Round Moat, the remains of a Saxon settlement from at least 250 years before Domesday. This is unlikely to be the original settlement.

Individuals who have left their mark on local maps include William de Mortuo Mari, who was at Mortimer's Farm in 1298, while Wildbores Farm was worked by John Wellbore, son of Phillip Wellbore, in 1640.

Foxton

Domesday records this name as Foxetune, which comes from Old English *fox tun* and is easy to see as 'the farmstead where foxes are seen'.

The local pub shows support for the royal House of Hanover in the White Horse.

Fulbourn

Documented as Fuulburne in 1050 and as Fuleberne in 1086, this comes from Old English *fugal burna* and describes 'the stream frequented by birds'.

Wool Street instantly brings to mind the image of sheep, so perhaps this is a drovers road where those animals were taken to market. However the real origin is quite the opposite, literally a wolf in sheep's clothing for this indeed describes 'where wolves are seen'.

Bishop's Charity Farm originally amounted to one croft and 63 acres of land which were given for the benefit of the poor by the vicar of All Saints church 1458-76, still operating as the Rev Jeffrey Bishops Charity. Other individuals who have left their mark on the map are Joseph Butcher, who was at Butcher's Farm by 1806, Robert Wright was associated with Wright's Grove by 1403, and Cole's Green was home to the family of Robert Cole in 1279.

Pubs here include the White Hart, once the generic name for a pub much the same as 'hoover' is used for a vacuum cleaner. The Six Bells refers to the number of bells or peals from the local church. While the name of the Bakers Arms probably shows the alternative career of the landlord, many early inn-keepers doubled as the village baker and/or butcher.

G

Gamlingay

A name recorded in Domesday as Gamelingei, a solitary early record and one which makes it difficult to see the true origin. However we do know the alternatives for the three elements here, for example the suffix could either be *haeg* 'an enclosure' or *eg* 'dry ground in marsh'. The other unknown may seem minor, yet the different between *ing* and *inga* is important for both always follow a personal name and show whether the individual was present or not. This name perfectly illustrates this, for if this is *ing* then this is 'the *haeg/eg* associated with a man called Gamela', yet *inga* would give 'the *haeg/eg* of the family or followers of a man called Gamela'.

Dennis Green is not the person but the place, the individual concerned is Thomas Dennis who was here by 1672. Field names include those which have very clear beginnings, such as the soil seen in the name of the Sands. Others are less evident, such as the Old Scandinavian *holmr* referring to 'the raised drier ground in the marsh' which is the suffix for many place names. Here Welleses Holme, Cloptons Holme and Maggot's Holme sees *holmr* following the names of those who owned these parcels of land in medieval times.

The growing of crops and similar uses gave names to Walnut Close, Bean Lands, Peasland, Wool Lands, and Willowbed Furlong. While the names of Broom Close, Rush Furlong, Thistle Lands, Water Lands Furlong, Puddle Furlong, Stonehill, Diche Furlong, and Clay Croft tell what we should expect to see. The suffixes here include furlong, a measurement of length known to horseracing enthusiasts as equal to 220 yards and derived from two Old English words *furh* 'furrow' and *lang* 'long'. This length was not standardised until around 1300 and historically was another of those indeterminate measurements based on a seemingly unquantifiable and quite random event. This took the length a team of oxen with the ploughman could pull the plough before requiring a rest. When standardised it was settled at one-eighth of a mile and comprised of ten chains (the length of a cricket pitch from stumps to stumps). An area one furlong in length and one chain in width, ie 4840 square yards, was deemed the standard for the basic measurement of farmland, the acre – a measurement still commonly used today even though the UK is officially using the decimal system.

With Gamlingay being on the main coaching route to London, landlords were quick to tap this potential revenue. Indeed it is claimed that at one time no less than 54 inns were open to the public at the height of the coaching era.

Gidding (Great, Little and Steeple)

Three places separated by only a mile which are found as Geddinge in 1086, Magna Giddinge in 1220, Gydding Parva in 1250, and Stepelgedding in 1260. All three will have a common origin from a Saxon personal name and Old English *ingas* giving the '(settlement) of the family or followers of a man called Gydda'. Here the distinguishing additions are from Latin *magna* meaning 'Great', Latin *parva* or 'Little', and Old English *stepel* or 'Steeple' and a reference to the church.

Great Gidding has the Fox & Hounds, a pub name which is easily seen as a hunting reference.

Girton

Records of this name include Grittune in 1060 and Gretone in Domesday. Here the name is derived from Old English *greot tun* which describes 'the farmstead on gravelly ground'.

Local names include Howhill Farm, where the first element of the name is more likely to be from *haugr* than *hoh* and thus 'the barrow on the hill'. From 1633 there is a record of a Robert Cole, who was associated with Cole's Plantation.

Pubs here include the Old Crown which shows allegiance to the monarchy; similarly the George could refer to any of the six kings of England, particularly the first four whose consecutive reigns lasted a total of 116 years; and the Travellers Rest, which offers a rest, food and a drink for those who pass by.

The village is also one of the few places in England where the black squirrel can be found. This is not a distinct species but simply a variation of the grey squirrel, literally one with a darker fur. While the occasional black squirrel can occur in litters of grey, here that rarity has become much more common and black squirrels may even be more populous than grey – it is difficult to say for certain for greys are naturally easier to spot in a visual survey.

Glatton

Records of this name include Domesday's Glatune, a name from Old English *glaed tun* which tells us it was known as 'the pleasant farmstead'.

Glinton

A name from Old English *glind tun* which tells us it was 'the fenced farmstead'. Here records of this place name are found as Clinton in 1060 and Glintone in Domesday.

The pub is the Blue Bell, undoubtedly showing this pub had strong connections with the church for the addition of 'blue' here shows a link to Christianity.

Godmanchester

The only record of note we have is from Domesday as Godmundcestre in 1086. Here is a Saxon personal name followed by Old English *ceaster* and referring to 'the Roman stronghold of a man called Godmund'.

The Romans knew their settlement as Durovigutum. Here the two elements, *duro* is actually a word from the Celtic cultures meaning 'strength', while the suffix is possibly Latin *vigeo* 'lively, thrive'. Hence this is possibly 'the thriving strongpoint'. Clearly there is no link between the Saxon and Roman names and there is no evidence to suggest the Saxon community ever used Roman constructions, indeed there is every reason to believe such would have been in ruin by the time the Saxons settled here. However there is evidence, both in the name and archaeologically, to show the Romans and Celts lived side by side. Once seen as Roman domination of the British, today it is viewed as a Romano-British culture.

The Via Devana is a road which sounds like an original Roman name, however nothing could be further from the truth. Unusually we know exactly when this name was coined and why. In 1825, Dr Mason, a Professor of Geology, thought he saw a Roman road running to here from Colchester in Essex. This name is from the eventual destination of Chester, a city second only in importance to London for the Romans was known by them as Deva. Whether the route exists or not is difficult to say, physical evidence is sketchy, particularly in the northern parts, while the route is not the arrow-straight line associated with such roads. The scepticism which initially greeted the claim was understandable, however in recent years his route has become accepted by most authorities. Today it is seen, not as a single route, but one linking other Roman roads, having junctions with the Watling Street at Mancetter in Warwickshire, the Fosse Way in the city of Leicester, and the Ermine Street here at Godmanchester.

The Black Bull is either an heraldic sign or a well known local beast, the Exhibition remembers the Great Exhibition at the Crystal Palace in 1851, and the White Hart was once the generic name for a pub, after it had first been used to represent Richard II.

Until 1975 there was only one bridge crossing the river, the aptly named Old Bridge. Today there are three, Old Bridge carries light traffic alongside a footbridge, while a modern road bridge spans the river and takes the by-pass. There is also the Chinese Bridge connecting the town to the water meadow. Legend maintained this bridge was built without the use of any metal fastenings, a claim which fascinated one architect and he was anxious to discover how this was achieved. Eventual permission was granted for him to dismantle the bridge to reverse engineer the technology. Having done so they then attempted to reassemble it simply by leaning and supporting itself under its own weight. Yet no matter what they attempted the bridge would not stand up on its own and had to resort to using nails to hold it together. It is now known that the legend was simply that and nails had been used originally. That none could be seen was entirely due to the visible metal nails having rusted and eroded away.

Grafham

Recorded in Domesday exactly as it is today, this name comes from Old English and is either *graf ham* or *graf hamm*. If the former is correct this is 'the homestead associated with a grove', while the latter would give 'the grove in the hemmed in land'.

Gransden (Great and Little)

Two places separated by under half a mile, the name is found as Grantandene in 973 and Grantesdene in 1086. Here the name means 'the valley of a man called Granta or Grante' from Old English *denu*. The Gransden Brook here is named from the place.

Little Gransden has Fuller's Hill Farm, which remembers 1780 when John Fuller was working this land. Hayley Wood is derived from *haeg leah* 'the enclosure of the woodland clearing'.

Granta, River

A name recorded as Gronte fluminis in 745, Grantan stream in 1000, Grentam in the twelfth century, and Graunte in 1608. This is also known as the Cam, and in places the Old River and even the Stapleford River, the first two are discussed under the relevant entries and the latter back-formation from that place name. This is a river name which once applied to a specific area as 'the fen river' or 'muddy river'.

Grantchester

Domesday lists this name as Granteseta, a name describing 'the settlers on the River Granta'. Here the Celtic river name is followed by Old English *saete*, the river name being discussed under its own entry.

Local names include Lacies Farm, named after the family of Henry de Lacy who were here by 1285; while there really was a family called Haggis working Haggis Farm in 1758.

The Blue Ball was once used as a pub sign to illustrate it was regularly visited by fortune tellers. Diversely it was also used in the coat of arms of the Courtenay family, earls of Devon, however this is rarely found outside the West Country. The Green Man is an image often shown as a Robin Hood figure, however it actually refers to the foresters or woodsmen. The Red Lion is the most common name in England, ironically most often referring heraldically to Scotland or Scotsmen.

The poem which begins: "If I should die think only this of me, that there's some corner of a foreign field that is forever England," was written by Rupert Brooke. The Rupert Brooke public house here was named for another of his works entitled *The Old Vicarage, Grantchester*. The village has a number of odd claims and references. It is said to have the highest concentration of Nobel Prize winners anywhere in the world, presumably these represent former academicians from the university town nearby. Byron's Pool is named after Lord Byron, it is reputed to have been where he swam.

Graveley

A name recorded as Greflea in the tenth century and as Gravelei in Domesday. Here is a name from Old English *graef leah* and referring to 'the woodland clearing by the pit or trench'.

Whether Roman Way is an original Roman road or even one which existed before the Empire's arrival, it is not the culture thatt makes this a significant route. Here the road forms part of the parish boundary, and the traditional county boundary, between Graveley and Offord Darcy in Huntingdonshire.

Great Staughton

With records of Stoctun in 1000 and Tochestone in 1086, here is a basic name from Old English *stoc tun* or the 'farmstead at an outlying hamlet'. The addition is to distinguish this from Little Staughton, which is to be found in Bedfordshire.

The locals are in no doubt where to enjoy a pint at a pub named the Tavern on the Green; while the White Hart originally symbolised Richard II but later became the generic name for any pub.

The local parish church is the only one in the county which boasts a square spire.

Grunty Fen

Early records of this name include Gruntifenn in 1221, as Gruntyngfenfelde in 1370, and as Grundefen in 1604. Here the term grunting is unknown, however it is thought to be related to either Norwegian *grumen* 'muddy' or Old Norse *grunnr* 'shallow', the topography certainly fits with a shallow place', which undoubtedly would have readily become muddy in wet weather. Nearby Grander's Grunty Fen and Grunty Fen Drain are minor place names derived from here.

Gunthorpe

Recorded as Gunetorp in 1130, this name is derived from Old Scandinavian where the personal name is followed by *thorp* and describes 'Gunni's outlying farmstead'.

Guyhin

Here is a name, found in 1275 as La Gyerne, which combines Old French *guie* and Old English *hyrne*. This refers to 'the guided angle or corner of land', this being where tidal flow was controlled to prevent salt water entering the system on every high tide.

Murrow gets its name from 'the row of cottages in a marsh'; Rummer's Farm is from Old English *ruh mere* 'the rough land by the pool'; and Nymandole Farm refers to the allocated land shared by nine men'.

The Oliver Twist is a pub with the name of the eponymous hero of the novel by Charles Dickens.

H

Haddenham

Listed as Haedan ham in 970 and as Hadreham in Domesday, this place name comes from Old English *ham* and a Saxon personal name which tells of 'Haeda's homestead'.

The Cherry Tree as a pub name would always refer to such being found nearby, thus acting as a signpost, especially in spring when the tree is in blossom. The Three Kings is a religious sign, a reminder of the Magi who visited the infant Christ at Bethlehem.

For over thirty years there has been a steam rally held here in early September. Attracting 20,000 visitors from all over the country, monies raised go to local causes and charities.

Haddenham Sign

Haddon

Both the record of Haddedun in 951 and as Adone in 1086, this name is seen as coming from a Saxon personal name and Old English *dun* and describes 'Headda's hill'.

Hail Weston

Seen in 1199 as Heilweston, the basic name here is among the most common in England. From Old English *west tun* this refers to 'the western farmstead' and was clearly named by a settlement to the east of here – although which will never be known. The addition is an earlier name of the River Kym, a Celtic name referring to 'the dirty stream'.

Hall Weston

As if to prove this is among the most common names in England, as stated under the previous entry, Weston, along with Norton and Sutton are found the length and breadth of the land. Weston comes from Old English *west tun* and describes 'the westerly farmstead', named such by a settlement east of here. Normally we would expect to find an addition and here it comes from the earlier Celtic name, itself derived from the former name for the River Kym and describing 'the dirty stream'.

Hamerton

Domesday records this name as Hambertone, a name which comes from Old English *hamor tun* and describes 'the farmstead where the plant hammer-sedge grows'.

Hardwick

A common place name, this example found as Hardwic in 1050 and as Harduic in 1086. The came comes from Old English *heorde wic* and refers to 'the specialised farm for herds'.

The Port Way is an ancient route linking the Cam Valley with Ermine Street. Probably pre-Roman, this name tells us it comes from *port* meaning 'market'. The public house here is the Blue Lion which, as with the vast majority of coloured names, is heraldic. As the image is so unusual, for once we know the source. This refers to the Danish royal family, in particular Queen Anne (1574-1619), wife of James I and mother of Charles I.

Modern developers have named roads to remember the trees which were removed to make way for the buildings. Hence we find Worcester Avenue, Bramley Way, Pippin Walk, Limes Road, Ellison Lane, Quince Road, Laxton Avenue, Russet Walk, and Blenheim Way.

Harlton

Recorded in Domesday as Herletone, this place name features a Saxon personal name and Old English *tun* which refers to 'Herela's farmstead'.

Butler's Spinney is a reminder of Peter le Bouteillier, who was here by 1232.

The local is the Hare and Hounds, a reminder of the traditional sport and quite possibly a pub where the hounds were kennelled.

Harston

A similar name to the previous entry and one with a similar meaning. Here the name is found as Herlestone in 1086, this comes from a Saxon personal name and Old English *tun* and refers to 'Herel's farmstead'.

Baggot Hall has many early records and yet none give any clue as to the origin of the name. However perhaps it is simply a corruption of the nearby Maggots Mount, as seen in 1825, which today is known as St Margaret's Mount. While Margarets today would probably not appreciate it, in those days 'Maggot' was a popular pet name for those christened Margaret.

Local pubs include the common names such as that showing royal support at the Queens Head, while advertising the chance to have one's horse shod gave rise to the Three Horseshoes. However not all the names are so common, for example the Pemberton Arms is named after the family who had their home at nearby Trumpington for several hundred years, and the Old English Gentleman reminds us of the importance of attracting a good class, and of course affluent, customer for it adds to the reputation of the premises.

Hartford

Domesday's record of Hereforde shows this is derived from Old English *here ford* and describes 'the ford suitable for the passage of an army'. It hardly seems likely this was created specifically for an army, thus this should be understood as meaning it is wider than normal and is very hard wearing.

Local pubs range from that which is obviously a reference to the brewing industry in the Barley Mow, a 'mow' is a stack or sheaf of barley and an indication that beer was brewed here, while there is also the very unusual name of the King of the Belgians. There are two potential links with England and the Belgian monarchy, the earliest is also the least likely origin. Leopold I married Princess Charlotte, the daughter of George IV of England, but her death in

Haddenham Sign

1817 came fourteen years before he ascended to the throne. Hence we look forward to Albert I (1875-1934), a popular figure for his democratic outlook and for his inspirational role as head of the resistance against the Germans in the First World War.

Haslingfield

Found in the Domesday survey as Haslingefeld, this name has two possible meanings. If this is from a Saxon personal name and Old English *inga feld*, then we are seeing 'the open land of the family or followers of Haesela'. However if this comes from *haesling feld* then this is 'the open land where hazel trees grow'.

The Mareway is a name derived from Old English *maere weg*. Meaning 'the boundary way', it comes as no surprise to find this place on the parish boundary. Another part of this route is known as Potters Way, an indication this was a route used by 'makers of pots' and one which would have been used by them for some time in order for the name to stick.

Other names found here include Chapel Hill, which is the only reminder of the chapel here dedicated to the Virgin Mary. Frog End does not refer directly to the amphibian, this is a nickname for a permanently marshy spot. Money Hill is named from the tumulus here, likely the supposed site of a fabulous treasure.

Cantelupe Farm is a comparatively recent name, a reminder of Viscount Cantelupe, son of the Earl de la Warr, who had holdings here in the early nineteenth century. The 12th baron, Thomas West, was governor of the Jamestown Colony where he was known as Lord Delaware. The Delaware Bay was named after him and thereafter the state of Delaware, the Delaware River and tribe of the Delaware Indians, with many other counties, towns, streets and buildings also taking his name.

Imagery is all important in pub signs and thus names. Flowers are ideal subjects and none feature more in pub names than the rose, it also has the benefit of being a patriotic image as it symbolises England. There are many slight changes to this basic name but all carry the same message, here the local is the Little Rose.

Hatley (East and St George)

Two places less than a mile apart which share a common origin from Old English *haett leah* to refer to 'the woodland clearing on or by a hill'. These names are recorded as Hatelai in 1086, as Esthatteleia in 1199, and as

Hattele de Sancto Georgio in 1279. These additions comes from *east* telling us it is 'easterly' in comparison with that held by the family of Sancto Georgio, who were here by the thirteenth century. There was also the uncultivated part still known as Hatley Wilds.

Hauxton

Records of this name include Hafucestune in 975 and Hauochestun in 1086. Here is a name from a Saxon personal name and Old English *tun* describing 'Hafoc's farmstead'.

The local pub is the Rose, an image which is synonymous with the English nation and thus a patriotic symbol.

Helpston

Listed as Hylpestun in 948, this name is derived from a Saxon personal name and Old English *tun*, which speaks of the 'farmstead of a man called Help'.

Hemingford (Abbots and Grey)

Records of this place name include Hemmingeford in 974, Emingeford in 1086, Hemingford Abbatis in 1276, and Hemingford Grey in 1316. Here the name comes from Old English *inga ford* and a Saxon personal name, giving 'the ford associated with the family or followers of a man called Hemma or Hemmi'. The additions are both manorial, showing early possession by the Abbot of Ramsey and the family of De Grey, respectively.

At Hemingford Abbots we find the Axe & Compass, a name derived from its two earlier names. Originally the area around here was all woodland and the pub was the Foresters Arms, later it became the Carpenters Arms, and now it features the tools of the woodsman and the carpenter. At Hemingford Grey the local is the Cock Inn, most often a sign indicating this was a venue for cock-fighting.

Heydon

A name which may take either of two possible Old English beginnings, the name recorded as Haidenam in Domesday in 1086. Here is either *heg denu* and 'the valley where hay is made' or from *haeg denu* and 'the valley with an enclosure'. Unless further examples are found, it seems unlikely if we shall ever know which is the true origin.

Hildersham

Listed as Hildricesham in the Domesday record of 1086, here is 'the homestead of a man called Hildric' and which features an Old English *ham* and a Saxon personal name.

The name of Alder Carr is a hybrid of a Saxon and a Scandinavian name, in that order, and describes 'the alder tree marshland'. Burgoyne's Plantation remembers 1427, when John Burgoyn was living here. Another prominent tree was a pointer to the local pub, at one time that tree stood outside the Pear Tree public house.

The Benedictine monk, English chronicler, artist of illuminated manuscripts, and cartographer Matthew Paris (1200-59) is believed to have been born in the village. Later the eighteenth century clergyman and writer Conyers Middleton spent time here.

Hilton

A name from Old English *hyll tun* and referring to 'the farmstead by a hill'. This name is found as Hiltone in 1196.

The Prince of Wales public house most often refers to the son of Queen Victoria, later Edward VII, who held the title longer than anyone until that record was surpassed by the present incumbent, Prince Charles.

The village green contains a turf maze with a stone pillar in the centre telling exactly who constructed this figure. William Sparrow (1641-1729) is said to have cut the turf maze in 1660. Approximately 55 feet in diameter it is thought to be based on a paved construction in Chartres Cathedral.

Hinxton

Domesday records this name as Hestitone, a name from a Saxon personal name preceding Old English *ing tun* and referring to 'the farmstead associated with a man called Hengest'.

Histon

This name is recorded as Histone in Domesday, when it was taxed for its three watermills. Here the name comes from Old English *hysse tun* and refers to 'the farmstead of the young men'.

Bower's Farm is a simple name to define, being associated with John Bowyer by 1640. Much less obvious is the name of Camping Close which, even if we know it means 'place for contending a camp ball', still reveals little. This is the site of a football match, probably an annual event, but this is not the beautiful game, something more akin to the organised melee famously played through the streets of Ashbourne in Derbyshire every Shrove Tuesday.

Pub names here include the King William IV, showing allegiance to the monarchy in general, rather than specifically this king. The Red Lion is an heraldic reference to Scotland. The Boot Inn is a simple visual sign which increased in popularity following each victory of the Duke of Wellington. The Barley Mow refers to the stack of barley, a very obvious indication that beer was on offer.

The present mill was built in the eighteenth century and, after falling into disrepair, was restored and is now a visitor attraction. There is a mill mentioned in Domesday and it seems certain this occupied exactly the same position. Gun's Lane is named after a local family. On the village sign is a man wearing a hat who is holding a rock over his head, this rock is now seen in the gardens of the Boot Inn. It was to this public house, his preferred drinking establishment, that Moses Carter carried the stone from its location at the building site to where it still rests today. Carter lived in the village all his life (1801-60), hence he was known as the Histon Giant, an apt name if he really was his reputed seven feet tall.

Hobson's Brook

A tributary of the Cam where the earliest reference is as Hobson's Watercourse in 1625, probably related to Thomas Hobson a carrier from Cambridge who also gave his name to Hobson Street.

Hoffer Brook

This tributary of the Cam is found as Hoppeforthebroc in 1308, as Hoppefordebroke in 1323, as Horforthbroke in 1540, and as Hoffer Brook for the first time in 1757. There is also a Hoffer Bridge, where records are rather earlier and more numerous, which are as uncertain as the name of the brook itself. However the bridge does seem to be derived from an early name for the ford as Appelewellasford which tells us it was 'the ford of the apple tree stream'.

Holme

A name from old Scandinavian *holmr* which is found as Hulmo in 1167, this name refers to 'the dry ground in a marsh'.

Within the parish is a region which was measured as 9.8 feet below sea level, making it the lowest point on mainland Britain.

Holywell

A name recorded as Haliewelle in 1086, the Domesday record showing this comes from Old English *halig wella* and referring to 'the holy spring or stream'.

The Ferry Boat Inn, named because of its waterside location, is one of several pubs in England which claims to be the oldest. Indeed it is said it was built on top of the grave of a local girl who committed suicide near the parish church during the reign of Edward the Confessor in 1050. It is held that the girl took her own life when jilted by the local woodcutter. Inside the inn there is a stone slab making up part of the floor, it is said to court ill luck to walk upon it. Held to be where the ghost of this young girl rises from the slab on March 17th each year, the anniversary of her death, the apparition then glides away towards the riverbank where the ferry would have collected and dropped its passengers.

The story attracted paranormal investigators and a seance was conducted during the 1950s. From there it was revealed the girl was one Juliet Tewsley, while the identity of the woodcutter was Thomas Zoul. The following year another seance, presumably not by the same team, gave the date of her death as the fifteenth century.

Home Dole Brook

This minor stream feeds into the Gransden Brook and takes its name from Old English *holm dal* and means 'the dry land in the valley'.

Horningsea

Records of this name include Horninges ige in 975 and as Horningesie in 1086. Here this is either a Saxon personal name with Old English *eg* and referring to 'Horning's dry ground in a marsh', or from *horning eg* which would be 'the dry ground in a marsh at the horn-shaped hill'.

Clayhithe comes from *claeg hyth*, telling us it was 'the landing place on the clay'; Eye Hall Farm was known for its 'well watered land'; Kings Farm is named after the man who was here, Rogerus le Kyng; and Snouts

Corner is a topographical name, referring to 'the projecting drier land in the fen'.

The Plough and Fleece takes its name from its rural location, referring to agriculture and the rearing of sheep. The Crown is a common pub name, so much so that an addition found in the name of the Crown and Punchbowl, the addition an advertisement for drink.

Horseheath

It seems impossible that this name could mean anything other than 'the heath where horses are kept'. Indeed the records of Horseda in 1080 and Horsei in 1086 show this does mean such, it is even still possible to recognise this in the original Old English *hors haeth*.

Local people and places come together in the names of Cardinal's Green and Limberhurst Farm, named from Peter Carbonel and John de Lymbery who were here by 1268 and 1272 respectively.

The local pub is the Old Red Lion, an heraldic image most often referring to Scotland but earlier signs could represent John of Gaunt. The addition of 'Old' is often misleading, many are not particularly old and the name more often should be seen as 'older'.

Houghton

A common name which almost always comes from Old English *hoh tun* and refers to 'the farmstead on a ridge or hill spur'. The name is found in Domesday as Hoctune in 1086.

The Three Horseshoes shows the pub had a blacksmith, together the two premises offered the same as the modern motorway service station. While four may seem a more logical number, it does make more sense if seen as a question, Three Horseshoes?

Famous former residents here include artist Charles Whymper; Potto Brown (1797-1871), a local miller and noncomformist philanthropist whose statue still stands in the village. Lastly we

Houghton and Wyton sign

come to Captain John Leslie Green (1888-1916), who was awarded the Victoria Cross for his actions at the Battle of Loos when, although wounded himself, went to aid a fellow officer who had also been wounded and was caught on the barbed wire defences. Dragging the injured man to the comparative shelter of a shell hole, he dressed the man's wounds as grenades, bombs and bullets were continually aimed in their direction. John Green then set about getting his fellow officer to safety and, having almost reached his goal, was himself killed.

Huntingdon

A name found as Huntandun in 973 and as Huntedun in 1086, the name is certainly Old English but it is difficult to be certain how the first element is being used. If this is *hunta dun* then this is 'the hill of the huntsman', however perhaps this represents a personal name and thus is 'Hunta's hill'.

This also represents an old county name, one which became officially a part of Cambridgeshire in 1974 but, as with many boundary changes at that time, failed to be recognised by many. Despite several attempts to get the county recognised over the last four decades it remains a part of Cambridgeshire. As with many counties, this name takes that of the county town and adds Old English *scir* which was a Saxon term describing an 'administrative district'.

Street names include George Street, St Germain Street, and St Peter's Road, all of which were named from the churches here. Cowper Road is named after the poet William Cowper, described as a horrible unbalanced individual at the time, he would have later been identified as a manic depressive. American Lane is named such for being in the most remote part of the parish, while this theme later inspired the name of California Road.

Lammas Gardens is one of the many in England derived from the field name, itself named from Lammas Day or 1st August. This would have been the field which provided the wheat crop to produce the first loaf of that season, one joyously brought to the church as part of the Lammas Day ceremonies.

Like all towns newer developments in Huntingdon have themes. Trees were the inspiration behind Beech Close, Ash Close, Elm Close, and Chestnut Close. Characters from Shakespeare are seen in Prospero Way, Hamlet Close, Oberon Close, Othello Close, Falstaff Way, and Duncan Way. While famous sailors are seen in Drake Close, Nelson Road, Rodney Road, Frobisher Close, and Hardy Close.

Chequers Court is named after the Chequers Public House, one of the oldest of pub names it original spoke of the board game being played here. Later it was also used to refer to a moneyer, and is still used as such in the office of the man charged with looking after the finances of the nation, the Chancellor of the Exchequer.

Of course the town would not be complete without one of its most famous residents, remembered by Cromwell Walk. The man is also seen in the pub names of Cromwells Cafe Bar and the Lord Protector. The name of the Golden Knight was a nickname held by the sixteenth century knight Sir Henry Cromwell. Other famous people were honoured by the naming of the Victoria Inn, after Queen Victoria; the Prince of Wales, most often refers to the future Edward VII; Samuel Pepys is after the famous diarist, although during his lifetime he was an important naval official; and the Montagu Arms is named after the family who were Earls of Huntingdon.

Birds make for excellent imagery and are therefore perfect for the pub sign. Here we find examples of birds of prey given to three pubs known as the Hawk, Harrier, and Falcon. The Sun is a simple sign and one where the suggestion of warmth is seen as a welcoming image. Names taken from the locality include the Old Bridge Hotel, Alconbury Mill and the Market Inn, while the Three Tuns is named for the arms of the Worshipful Company of Vintners. The Three Compasses is heraldic, referring to use by the guilds of the three most important construction trades, masons, carpenters and joiners.

Local legend tells of the haunting of Hinchingbrooke House, a former convent. From the nearby Nun's Bridge over Alconbury Brook have come reports of hauntings by a nun from the convent. She is not alone but is said to be accompanied by another figure who appears to be a nurse. It is said that the nun had a lover, a monk, and their liaisons resulted in them both being murdered.

Huntingdonshire

Now a part of Cambridgeshire, this historic county included the towns of St Ives, St Neots, and Godmanchester. As with so many other counties, this features the name of the county town with the addition of Old English *scir* or 'district'. Again, like other counties, this is first recorded in the tenth century and remained largely unchanged until the late nineteenth century.

The county flag of Huntingdonshire, ironically not officially introduced until 2009 by which time it had been in and out of existence to some degree or other for over thirty years. However the flag is much older. Described as "A banner Vert charged with a Hunting Horn stringed Or" – today a green flag with a gold horn tied with a ribbon – it was granted by the College of Arms. It is particularly evident on 25th April, Huntingdonshire Day, chosen for it was the birth date of probably the county's most famous son, Oliver Cromwell.

The crest of arms of Huntingdonshire are used and indeed owned by Huntingdonshire District Council. This is not unusual, no county has an official coat of arms, each is privately owned. Yet this did not stop an imaginative image being created. A basic lozenge represents the roughly diamond-shaped county, split into two halves: the top three sheaves showing this is primarily agricultural land, the lower half featuring the hunting horn representing the county name. The top of the crest has a red lion, said to represent the Scottish monarchs who were also earls of Huntingdon. While no proof this was ever used by the Scots south of the border has been traced, there is no doubting it is referred to indirectly again and again for the most popular pub name in England, the Red Lion, ironically refers to Scotland.

I

Ickleton

Recorded as Icelingtune in 975 and as Hichelintone in 1086, this name is derived from a Saxon personal name and Old English *ing tun* which speaks of this as 'the farmstead associated with a man called Icel'.

Brookhamton can still be seen as 'the homestead by a brook'; Caploe Hill comes from *copphlaw* or 'the rounded hill'; Norman Hall was home to Peter and John Norman in 1327; Vallence Farm was associated with Giles and Agnes de Valence by 1285; and Abbey Farm and The Caldrees are both derived from being held by the Abbey of Calder in Cumbria from at least 1254.

Icknield Way

What is generally regarded as a Roman road is known to have existed prior to the arrival of the great empire, possibly even before the founding of Rome itself. This name appears as Iccenhilde weg in 903, as Ichenild in 1250, Hikenuldstrate in 1225, Hykenhilte in 1274, and as Ykenildes Weye in 1279. This is undoubtedly a Celtic or earlier British road name and probably, as with the other major roads of Ermine Street and Watling Street, named at just one small part of its great length and eventually spreading to refer to all of it. Clearly this name has changed little in 1,200 years, and probably twice as long, and yet without further evidence the meaning is unknown.

One part of the road is known as Holloway, a common name found along many popular and ancient routes. This refers to a place literally worn away by the constant passage of traffic over centuries. Another section is referred to as Mereways, from Old English *maere weg* 'the boundary way', where it follows a parish boundary.

Impington

With records of Impintune in 1050 and as Epintone in 1086, here is a name from a Saxon personal name and Old English *ing tun* which informs us it was 'the farmstead associated with a man called Empa or Impa'.

Howe House is derived from Old English *hoh* and describes the '(place at) the hill spur', while Burgoynes Farm took the name of the family represented by John Burgoyn here in 1429.

Two pubs here, the Rose and Crown has two symbols which refers to England and its monarch, hence a patriotic establishment. The coming of the railways fuelled the growth in the number of pubs or hotels to offer accommodation and refreshment to these early travellers. Ever since its early days the Railway Vue has stood at the apex formed where New Road meets Station Road, two roads which together point to the level crossing and the railway. The name here is self-explanatory, although why it developed as Vue and not View has never been clear.

The former Impington Hall was built from 1580 by John Pepys, great-uncle of the famous diarist Samuel Pepys. A disastrous fire in 1953 resulted in the building being condemned as dangerous. Impington was the first home of the Chivers factory at the Victoria Works where their original product of jam was soon accompanied by marmalade and, probably their most famous product, Chivers Jellies. The farm and estates included the village's most prominent feature, its windmill, originally built in 1806.

Isleham

A name telling us it was 'the homestead associated with a man called Hisla', where the Saxon personal name is found with Old English *ing ham*. The name appears as Gisleham in Domesday, with an earlier record from 895 as Yselham.

Spooner's Drove was named after the family of William Spooner, who were here by 1780, while The Temple is a reminder of the messuage held by the Master of the Templars in England by 1279.

As much as the image of the Rising Sun promises the warmth of the new day, it also suggests the warmest of welcomes, hence it being chosen by so many important families and individuals such as Edward III and Richard III. Another popular heraldic image is that of the fabulous beast held to be the result of crossing the lion and the eagle, the king of beasts and the most magnificent of birds, thus the name of the Griffin. The Merry Monk shows there is a link between the local pub and the church and the promise of a good time to be had by all.

The local earthwork known as Devil's Dyke has been studied for many years. Archaeologists have uncovered relics from Saxon, Roman, Iron Age, Bronze Age, and Stone Age occupation. Findings included the Isleham

Hoard, an amazing collection of 6,500 pieces of bronze dating from the late Bronze Age. Devil's Dyke has no religious or satanic connections but is simply born of numerous stories told over many, many centuries.

K

Kennett
A place name which comes from the river of this name, a Celtic river name discussed under its own entry. The place is recorded as Chenet in Domesday, when it was held by Nicholas from William de Warenne.

Kennet, River
This particular Kennet is a tributary of the Lark, there are also rivers of this name in Berkshire, Westmorland and Lancashire. All are of Celtic origin, possibly *kun* or Welsh *cwn* and thus named from the 'top, summit' from whence the river springs. However this example, being in the very flat fenland, is difficult to see as having any 'summit' even though there is an incline for water simply must flow downhill this would have been hard for our ancestors to see. The earliest record of this dates from 1318 as Cheneteforde, itself referring to the river crossing rather than the river itself, and without other examples it seems unlikely this name will ever be understood with any certainty.

Keyston
Domesday's record of Chetelestan is the only early record of note. This comes from a combination of an Old Scandinavian personal name and Old English *stan*, together telling of 'the boundary stone of a man called Ketil'.

The Pheasant Inn features the colourful image of the bird introduced from Russia as a game bird and it is probably for this hunting element that it appears on pub names. Poet John Donne once owned the village rectory.

Kimbolton
A name which describes 'Cynebald's farmstead', and where the Saxon personal name is followed by Old English *tun*. The name is found in the pages of Domesday as Chenebaltone.

The name of the New Sun Inn indicates it is a newer building or a rebuild of an earlier inn named from the promise of a new dawn or beginning. The White Horse Inn symbolises the House of Hanover.

The present Kimbolton Castle is used by an independent school but is not the original building. Previously the building was home to Katherine of Aragon, first wife of Henry VIII following their divorce. The queen died here in 1536 and was taken to Peterborough Cathedral for burial.

Kingston

Listed as Chingestone and Kingestone in Domesday, as Kinkestune in 1218, and as Chinston in 1265, this tells us it was 'the king's or royal farmstead'.

Locally we find Armshold Farm, a part of the parish of Kingston which is on the Great Eversden side of the Armshold Lane, the traditional parish boundary. The name describes 'the hill of a man called Earning'.

Kirtling

Another name of Old English origin, here the Saxon personal name is followed by the element *ing*. Recorded as Chertelinge in 1086, this was 'the place associated with a man called Cyrtla'.

Upend is a local name which refers to the '(place of) the up dwellers' and was not strictly applied to the place itself. Pratt's Green Farm was worked by the family of John Prat in 1327, although the name of Lucy Wood is derived from *hlose haeg* meaning 'the enclosure of the pig sty'.

Knapwell

Found as Cnapwelle in 1045 and as Chenepewelle in Domesday, this is either Old English *cnapa wella* and 'the spring or stream of the servant' or the first element is a Saxon personal name and thus 'Cnapa's spring or stream'.

Kneesworth

The earliest surviving record of this name is as Cnesworth in 1218, this comes from a Saxon personal name and Old English *worth* and describes 'Cyneheah's enclosure'. The name of Mills Farm marks the position of the former Kneesworth Mill.

L

Lady Nunn's Old Eau

A name for that part of the Old South Eau between Grange Hill and Cloughs Cross, a part of the border with Lincolnshire which is why it is seen as The Shire Drain in 1632 with earlier records of Lady Nunns Ee in 1600 and later as Lady Nunns Eay in 1706. The religious reference is not what it seems, this is a personal name referring to the association with Lady Nunn, wife of Sir Edmund Noon who held land on the Lincolnshire bank.

Landbeach

Seen as Bece in 1086 and as Landebeche in 1218, the original name comes from Old English and is either *bece* which describes 'the valley stream' or *baec* 'the low ridge'. Later the addition of land distinguished this place from Waterbeach.

Local names include Frith Fen Drove or 'the drovers' road alongside the fen covered with brushwood'; Goose Hall must have been near where geese were regularly seen and probably driven down the road here; and Worts Farm is a reminder of the family of William Worts who are recorded here in 1709.

Landwade

The eleventh century record of Landuuade shows this comes from Old English *land waed* and describes 'the district ford'.

Lark, River

A name which is probably an example of back-formation from Lackford. This tributary of the Ouse is found as Pryckewillowewayter in 1549, Mildenhall river of the dead mile in 1604, and Mildenhall streame in 1611, all these are from place names found along its banks.

Leighton Bromswold

A name which describes a scene from Saxon life, for the basic name describes a kitchen garden. Listed as Lectone in Domesday and as Letton super Bruneswald in 1254, this comes from Old English *leac tun* and describes 'the leek, garlic and/or herb enclosure'. The addition was originally a separate settlement, one from a Saxon personal name with Old English *weald* and meaning 'Brun's high forest land'. The name seems to have been mirrored in the local pub, the Green Man was originally a reference to the woodsmen or foresters.

This place name was also seen in the name of the local hundred, a basic administrative district in Saxon times. Known as Leightonstone the suffix refers to the marker stone, situated near the lych gate of the present parish church, the place where the moot court assembled to discuss matters such as collection of taxes, settle disputes, etc.

Leverington

The earliest known record is exactly as the present form in a document dated 1130. Here is a Saxon personal name and Old English *ing tun* and referring to 'the farmstead associated with a man called Leofhere'.

Minor names here include Bone's Gote, Old English *bonde* and Middle English *gote* together describing 'the peasant's watercourse'. Gorefield tells us it was 'the open land of the fen'; Spittle Field was an endowment of the Hospital of St John the Baptist; Wolf Lane is a corruption of *wyrm feld* 'the open land where snakes are numerous'; Wrat Field is from *wraett feld* 'the open land where crosswort grows'; Fitton Hall was built at 'the meadow land by a river'; and Wool Croft has no connection with sheep but describes 'Wilfa's croft'. Modern names include those of literary giants John Chaucer and John Milton, who proved the inspiration for Chaucer Close and Milton Drive.

The local pub is the Six Ringers, which has exactly the same origins as the many pubs called the Bell. It shows the close relationship between the pub and the church, for many years the only two meeting places for a community which spent most of the week spread across the land where they were working. Here the ringers refers to those who ring the bells and is a welcome variation on the usual 'bell'.

The image of the Rising Sun is used to suggest a new dawn, a change for the better. The image was used in the coat of arms of many families, including Edward III and Richard III.

Linton

Both records of Lintune in 1008 and Lintone in 1086 show this name comes from Old English *lin tun* and refers to 'the farmstead where flax is grown'.

Local names include Barham Hall, a name describing 'the enclosure on the hill'; Borley Wood comes from 'the woodland clearing on a hill'; Richard Payn was associated with Pain's Pasture by 1327; and it is difficult to see if the name of Mark's Grave is a name which refers to 'the grave at the crossroads' or 'the boundary grove'.

Local pubs include the Waggon and Horses, an indication that before the canals these large wheeled vehicles were the sole method of carrying heavy loads around the country. Such vehicles covered relatively short distances, dropping the load at public houses where the landlord would act as an agent for further distribution. It seems today the pubs of this name are the only places where the spelling 'waggon' is found, yet while 'wagon' is more often seen the English dictionary does prefer 'waggon'.

It is no surprise to find a pub with a name like Dog & Duck near water. This name could point to the royal sport of duck hunting, a particular favourite of Charles II. No gun and duck decoy for this monarch, dogs were sent in to the water to catch the birds who, having had their wings pinned, could only escape by diving. Pub names which date from after this particular pastime ended in the nineteenth century would refer to the more familiar method with a shotgun and retriever.

Litlington

With records of Litlingeton in 1183 and as Lidlingtone in 1086, this comes from Old English *ing tun* and a Saxon personal name, thus telling us it was 'the farmstead associated with a man called Lytel'.

Here is Chardle Ditch, this being the 'ditch with a cold spring' from *cald wielle*; from *lind hlaw* comes the name of Limlow Hill, the hill where lime trees grow'; D'Ovesdale Manor was home to John de Ovedale in 1304; and Rogerus de Huntingefeld was associated with Huntingefield Manor Farm in 1242.

Little Downham

This name is identical to that of Downham to the north and comes from Old English *dun ham* meaning 'the homestead on or by a hill'. Today Little Downham's population is much greater than Downham, although the area covered makes this name accurate.

Marshall Drove comes from *mersc healh* 'the marsh at the nook of land'. Pymore has two possible meanings, depending whether the first element is *peo* or *pie* giving 'the marshland infested by insects' and 'the marshland frequented by magpies'. However there can be no doubt as to the origins of California, this is an example of a remoteness name, and one which can almost be dated for the name did not exist until 1846 and was probably virtually unknown in Britain until the California Gold Rush began in 1848.

The local is the Plough, one of the most common pub names in England which dates from the days when the majority of the population worked the land. Strangely it did not become popular until as late as the sixteenth century.

Littleport

From Old English *lytel port* this name describes 'the small market town' The name was recorded as Litelport in Domesday, a possession of the Abbot of Ely who was taxed to the tune of 17,000 eels each year for this manor, eels were then an important food source.

Minor place names here include Apes Hall, nothing to do with primates, this tells us it was 'the aspen wood'. Similarly no ships of the desert will be seen along Camel Drove, this comes from *cam* 'crooked', the majority of 'droves' are arrow straight. Spaindelf Farm took the name of a very narrow dike for it is a derogatory term suggesting it was dug by a lazy person measuring only 'a span' literally a hand's breadth.

People who have left their mark on the local map are seen at Weltmore Farm, which is an early Saxon name describing 'Hwelp's marshland'. Later William Martin was associated with Martin's Drain by 1320, Alice Belle gave her name to Bell's Drove by 1327, John Horne's family were remembered by 1654 with Horn's Drove, Butcher's Hill Farm was worked by Edward Butcher by 1780, Thomas Cave was at Cave's Farm by 1840, the same year as Bates's Drove was associated with William Bates. Scotland Farm is not a family name, this tells us it was the farthest corner of this parish, referred to as a remoteness name.

The public houses of Littleport all rely on symbolism to convey a message. Sometimes the message is clear, as in the case of the Crown Inn showing support for the monarchy and thus a patriotic establishment. The Plough and Harrow features the two implements synonymous with the farmworker, the plough cuts the furrow while the harrow breaks the resulting larger clods and smooths out the ground. The Black Horse is less obvious, it is taken from a coat of arms but the symbol is so common it is well nigh impossible to suggest the origin.

Lode
A name found as Lada in the twelfth century, this name is derived from Old English *lad* which describes 'the water course, drainage channel'.

The local name of Anglesey seems unlikely to be 'the isle (dry land in marsh) of the Angles', hence this is probably from *anger healh* or 'the grassy nook of land'. Docking Droveway is a lane which describes 'the drovers' way where docks grow'. Individuals who are remembered in minor place names include Bull's Farm, Thomas le Bole was here in 1336, Harvey's Droveway, named after thirteenth century resident Simon fitz Heruey, and Thomas Hatley was associated with Hatley's Farm by 1814.

Locally we find Anglesey Abbey, home to the Fairhaven family. Today this National Trust property includes the attractive and unique grounds, with its restored watermill.

Lolworth
Found in 1034 as Lollesworthe and in 1086 as Lolesuuorde, this features a Saxon personal name and Old English *worth* to describe 'the enclosure of a man called Loll or Lull'.

Long Brook
A tributary of the Bourn Brook which is not recorded as such until 1825. This is not a particularly 'long' brook and is thus probably named in comparison with either another watercourse or, if it from a place name, a land feature.

Long Stanton
Found as simply Stantune in 1086 and later as Long Stanton in 1282, this comes from Old English *stan tun* and describes 'the farmstead near the standing stones'. The addition refers to the drawn out shape of the village aligned along the main road.

Locally we find the name of Long Stanton All Saints, after the dedication of the church on Church Lane. Similarly the dedication of the second church proved the inspiration of the name of Long Stanton St

Michael. Magdalene College Farm was a possession of the famous college, and Hatton's Road recalls the family headed by Sir Thomas Hatton who died in 1658.

The local pub is the Black Bull, which may be heraldic or simply a reference to a popular local beast.

Longstowe

Records of Stou in 1086 and as Lungestowe in 1268, this name comes from Old English *lang stow* and tells us it was 'the long place', that is aligned along the road.

One local pub is the Red House, a name which fits the colour of this building perfectly. A former pub here, built in 1865, was the Three Horseshoes Inn, a reminder of the days when the horse was the major form of transport and an advertisement for the blacksmith services alongside. However this particular establishment, which eventually closed in 2001, was renamed after the famous racehorse Golden Miller, trained by Basil Briscoe of Longstowe Hall. This horse, owned by Dorothy Paget, won the Cheltenham Gold Cup on three consecutive occasions (1932-5) and the Aintree Grand National in 1934. Many still argue this was the greatest steeplechaser of all.

M

Madingley

The Domesday record of Madeingelei in 1086 points to the being from a Saxon personal name and Old English *inga leah* and telling us of 'the woodland clearing of the family or followers of a man called Mada'.

A name which is self-explanatory is that of Moor Barns Farm, while Wrangling Corner is from Old English *wrang land* or 'the twisted strip of land'.

Madingley Hall, built by Sir John Hynde in 1543, was occupied by his family and descendants until the 1860s when Queen Victoria rented the property for the future Edward VII during his time as an undergraduate at Cambridge. The hall, its park and farmland have been owned by the University of Cambridge since 1948.

Manea

The earliest record of this name is as Oneia in 1177. This comes from Old English *eg*, 'the dry ground in marsh', with an uncertain first element which may be *maene* and suggesting it was held by the community. If Charles I had chosen Manea as the site for his new town in the seventeenth century the village would be renamed Charlemont, a name which would have needed no explanation.

Local names include Carroll's Farm, home to John Carrill by 1649, and Bond's Farm, worked by John Bond from at least 1819. Barnes's Drove is named after George Barnes, who held the position of Sergeant-at-Mace to the Bedford Level Corporation in 1663.

There are many names in the county which refer to Undertakers and Adventurers, names which refer to those who 'undertook' to dig the ditches and drains to dry out the fenland and those who 'undertook' to support the Undertakers while they did so. In return each Undertaker would receive an allocation of the newly reclaimed land, with the remainder shared pro rata between those who had financially backed the scheme. The local name of Charle Mont can be traced to a specific date at this time, 23rd July 1638, when fenmen were showing opposition to their apparently 'fair share' and Charles I declared himself sole Adventurer for the reclamation of the fenland, believing this would quell the opposition at a stroke.

March

Found in Domesday as Merche, this place name is derived from Old English *mearc* and tells us of 'the boundary place'.

Dartford Road does not lead to Dartford, however it does lead to 'the ford used by wild animals', the name coming from Old English *deor ford*. Burrow Moor speaks of it being 'the fishing weir by the stronghold', where wicker gates or traps would trap fish and provide a very rudimentary fish farming technique.

People are seen in the names of Clipson's Farm, home to John Clipson by 1771; Daintree Farm was worked by Jordan de Dauentre by 1260; Ralph Dod was working Dodd's Farm by 1251; Elizabeth Knighte was associated with Knight's End some time before 1688; Moore's Farm is a reminder that the family of Jonas Moore were here by 1669; Staffurth's Bridge took the name of Abraham Staffurth some time before 1818; and by 1669 Judey Wade had bequeathed Wade's Charity Farm for the benefit of the poor of the parish.

The Acre public house is in Acre Road, ultimately taking the name of a field here. The Coachmakers Arms shows the pub had facilities for the maintenance of the coach and horses; Hammer and Anvil is an alternative name showing a blacksmiths shop was available; King William IV is named after the somewhat unpopular monarch nicknamed the Sailor King; the Men of March show it catered for the locals; while the Seven Stars shows the constellation of Ursa Major or the Plough. The Golden Lion takes the name of the heraldic image which has been used to represent Henry I, although here it is more likely to be for the Percy family, dukes of Northumberland. A nation of patriots is the reason for the popularity of the Rose & Crown as a pub name, representative of England and its monarchy respectively. Royalty also brought the Red Lion image to England, for it most often represents Scotland and became the most common pub sign in England following the union between the two countries.

The local church is dedicated to St Wendreda, the only known dedication to this saint in the land. She was held to be the daughter of King Anna of East Anglia, a seventh century Saxon leader and one of the first to adopt Christianity, in which case her sisters were also canonised, Etheldreda became abbess of Ely and Sexburgha abbess of Minster-in-

Sheppey. Wendreda's relics were held in Ely Cathedral until 1016 when Edmund Ironside carried them into battle in the hope they would bring victory, however King Canute was victorious and presented the captured relics to Canterbury Cathedral. In 1343 they were returned to March but no mention is made of them since that date and thus are now considered lost.

Since 1979 students from Cambridge have walked from the town back to the city of Cambridge. This event, held in the third month of each year, is known as the March March march.

Marholm
Listed as Marham in 1060, this name is derived from Old English *mere ham* and refers to this as 'the homestead with or by a pond'.

Maxey
Here is a place name which combines an Old Scandinavian personal name and Old English *eg* which describes 'the dry ground in marsh of a man called Maccus'.

Melbourn
With records of Meldeburna in 970 and Melleburne in 1086, this name is seen as 'the stream where orach or a similar plant grows, coming from Old English *melde burna*.

There is still evidence of five burial mounds in Five Barrow Field; Hop Mallions is named as the valley associated with William and Alice Marioun in 1324; the family of James Muncey gave their name to Muncey's around 1840; and Noon's Folly Farm was home to Robert Noon in 1819, the 'folly' here from Old French *folie* 'leafy place' and suggesting a small plantation.

Meldreth
Found as Melrede in Domesday, this name is derived from Old English *myln ruth* and describes 'the stream with a mill'.

Mettle Hill gets its name from Old English *moot hlow* meaning 'the assembly hill'; and Chiswick End is a reminder that this was renowned for being 'the cheese farm'.

Mepal

From a Saxon personal name and Old English *halh*, this tells us of 'the nook of land of a man called Meapa', the name being recorded as Mepahala in the twelfth century.

Locally Cole's Farm recalls the family of William Cole who were here by 1840, while earlier in 1662 Samuel Fortrey was living near what is now known as Fortrey House. Here the inn is the Three Pickerels, this being a fish, specifically a young pike.

Mill River

Found as Le Metfeld in the fourteenth century this clearly was known for feeding at least one mill before heading off towards Litlington in Hertfordshire.

Milton

One of the most common place names in England, this is recorded as Middeltune in 975 and Middeltone in 1086. From Old English *middel tun* this tells us of 'the middle farmstead'.

Baits Bite Lock is on the River Cam, a name with three elements the last of which is self-explanatory. Old English *byht* means 'the curve or bend', while the first element is possibly the family name Bates.

Public houses are always keen to advertise their wares, the sign and thus the name is the obvious place to advertise and at Milton we find the Jolly Brewers. There is also the Lion and Lamb, another pub name with a religious reference for here the lion symbolises the Resurrection while the lamb is the Redeemer. The White Horse is taken from a coat of arms, most like representing one of the Guilds associated with public houses including Coachmen, Farriers, Innholders, Saddlers, and Wheelwrights.

Molesworth

Recorded by the Domesday clerics as Molesworde, this record tells us it was 'Mul's enclosure' where the Saxon personal name is followed by Old English *worth*.

In 1646 the whole of Europe was obsessed with finding and exterminating witches. Those sent out to seek such 'evils' descended on Molesworth and suspected John Winnick and Ellen Shepheard as being witches. No record of their guilt exists and thus we must assume they were considered innocent.

Morborne
A name coming from Old English *mor burna*, this describes 'the stream in a marshland'. The earliest record of this name is the of Morburne in Domesday.

Morden (Guilden and Steeple)
Records of this name include Mordune in 1015, Mordune in 1086, Gildene Morden in 1204, and as Stepelmordun in 1242. Here the basic name speaks of 'the hill in the marshland' from Old English *mor dun*. Here we find two such places separated by under a mile, hence the additions of *gylden* meaning 'wealthy, splendid' and *stepel* referring to the church steeple which could doubtless have been visible from a distance.

At Guilden Mordern we find Cobbs Lane, named after Thomas Cobbe who was here by 1339; Odsey takes its name from 'Odda's seath or pit, hole'; Ruddery End comes from *hryther rith* meaning 'cattle stream'; and one William Avenell was associated with the Avenels by 1301.

Steeple Morden has Gatley End, from *gata leah* 'the woodland clearing where goats are seen'; Browse Wood was associated with Hugo and Robert de Bruey in 1272; and Cheyney Lodge was home to William de Chaeny in 1248.

Murrow
Listed as Morrowe in 1376, this name is derived from Old English *mor raw* and tells us this was 'the row (of houses) in marshy ground'.

Muscat
An alternative name for Cat's Water, this name appears as Must in 1200, Musthea in 1350, Muscote Water in 1574, and The Murst in 1712. As the Cat's Water refers to a man called Catt, this clearly refers to the same person here related to a root word from which developed Middle English *mud*, Dutch *modder* and Old Norse *mykr* and thus 'the muddy place of Catt'.

N

Needingworth

A place name recorded as Neddingewurda in 1161, telling us of 'the enclosure of the family or followers of a man called Hnydda'. Here the Saxon personal name precedes Old English *inga worth*.

Nene, River

A river which flows from Northamptonshire, through Cambridgeshire to Norfolk, often overlooked but is ranked the ninth longest river in England. The Cambridgeshire stretch is recorded as Nen in 972, Nien in 1170, Neine flu in 1600, Neane in 1609, and Nyne in 1621, although below Wisbech once called the Wisbech Great River. There are some disagreements as to its origins, not helped by the differences in pronunciation – in Northamptonshire it is Nen, rhyming with 'men', while here it is Nean as in 'mean'. Suggestions that this refers to the 'nine springs' which form the source of the river seem unlikely given the Northamptonshire pronunciation, yet prior to accurate and up to date mapping rivers, and especially the longer rivers, could conceivably have different names every few miles. If this seems strange remember rivers age, from a fast-moving clear stream in its youth near the source, changing to a meandering sluggish course in middle age, down to the brackish waters of old age at its estuary with the sea. Furthermore there are changes along the banks too, woodland, marsh, cultivated land, settlements, fords, waterfalls, bridges, etc, all these and more have contributed to river names. In times when it was unusual to travel far from home they would be unlikely to know the river was known by other names, indeed even if they heard a different name they would not recognise it as referring to the same river. Hence a host of names for the one river is quite likely, making the pronunciation change between Cambridgeshire and Northamptonshire a possible indication these had quite separate origins.

As to the meaning of the name it is more likely to be from a Celtic tongue, especially considering the size and importance of this river, this would then speak of the Nene as the 'strong one' or similar.

New River
Not strictly a river in the natural sense, nor could it be considered new today. This was a channel cut in 1610 and known as 'new' from 1634.

Newark
Found in 1189 as Nieuyrk, this is derived from Old English *niwe weorc* and tells us it was 'the new fortification'.

Newton
Listed as Neutune in 1050, Nowetuna in 1120, Neotuna in 1150, and as Newenton in 1271, this is one of the most common English place names. As with all examples this is from *niwe tun* 'the newer farmstead', although it is surprising to find there is no distinguishing addition.

Locally we find Cockle Hill, Old English *hlaw* 'burial mound' following what is thought to be an unknown Middle English personal name.

The Queens Head is a clear show of support for the nation and the monarchy, a fine example of an image of Anne of Cleves. As the fourth wife of Henry VIII her marriage to the infamous Tudor monarch had little long term effect on her in comparison to his other wives. They married on 5th January 1540, despite the king's very vocal disappointment at her supposed beauty, yet by 24th June that year she had been asked to leave the court and by 6th July an annulment was sought and granted three days later. Anne did rather well out of the settlement, including acceptance into the king's family and known thereafter as the King's beloved sister. When she left the court, despite being of the German royal household, she never left her adopted England. Although she was only forty-one at the time of her death she managed to outlive her 'husband' and every other one of his wives.

Northborough
Even without the twelfth century record of Northburh it would still be easy to see this as coming from Old English *north burh* and describing 'the northern fortification'.

O

Oakington

The eleventh century Domesday survey records this name as Hochinton. Here a Saxon personal name with Old English *ing tun* and speaking of 'the farmstead associated with a man called Hocca'.

Coles Lane is named after Robert Cole who was living here by 1570, while Phyper's Farm remembers the family of John Phypers who worked this land by 1617.

The sign outside the White Horse public house would appear to be derived from the House of Hanover.

Offord (Cluny and Darcy)

Two places only half a mile apart and sharing a common origin in Old English *uppe ford* and describing 'the upper ford'. Records of this name include Upeforde and Opeforde in Domesday, as Offord Willemi Daci in 1220, and as Offord Cluyne in 1257. These additions are manorial, the parishes being held by the monks of Cluny Abbey in France and the Darcy family respectively.

At Offord Darcy we find the Horseshoe, this local pub is one of many in the land which would have advertised themselves as the motorway service station of its day. Some offered food or drink to satisfy the traveller, others concentrated on the mode of transport in the horse, here offering to replace any worn or lost shoes. The message becomes clearer if viewed as a question – Horseshoe? The Swan is a majestic bird favoured by many as a symbol in their coats of arms, including Henry VIII and Edward III, yet the vast majority of pubs take the name because it makes for a simple and attractive sign.

Old Croft River

A name not seen before 1606 which, despite the record of Old Craft River in 1830, is an example of back-formation from the Croft Hills. This is also the river which gave a name to Outwell and Upwell, for it was earlier known as the Aqua de Welle from the middle of the thirteenth century, *wielle* meaning simply 'river, stream'.

Old Hurst

Documented as Waldhirst in 1227, this name comes from Old English *wald hyrst* and describes 'the wooded hill by the forest'.

Old South Eau

There is no doubt this name means 'the old southern river', however why is more difficult to answer. Records of Old Southea in 1706 show it was 'old' compared to the New South Ea river, earlier it is the Southhea in 1387 where *ea* is 'river', although what this was 'south' of is a mystery unless it refers to it marking the southern boundary of Lincolnshire further east. In which case it will have been named by those living in Lincolnshire to the north.

Old West River

A tributary of the Cam, this name may define itself but is difficult to understand. Earlier it was referred to as Estee in 1302, a name meaning 'east river' and telling us it fed the Ouse from the east. Prior to this it was called Cotingelode 'the watercourse of Cotta's people', last listed as such in 1291. The modern name has been transferred from the West Water, a name discussed under its own entry, with the addition not because the name pre-dates it but because the banks are more eroded and less well defined.

Orton (Longueville and Waterville)

Two places separated by less than half a mile, hence the addition to a basic name derived from Old English and either *ufer tun* giving the 'higher farmstead' or perhaps *ofer tun* and the 'farmstead by a ridge or bank'. These places are found as Ofertune in 958, Ovretune in 1086, Ouerton Longavill in 1247, and as Ouertone Wateruile in 1248. Here the manorial affixes refer to these places being held by the Longauilla and the de Waltervilla families from the twelfth century.

At Orton Longueville we find the local pub named the Ramblewood Inn and, while there is no record of this as a local place name, there seems no other explanation to its origin unless it was created in order to make it appear to be an old place name, much as developers use street names to give the impression of a rural location today. The Botolph Arms takes its name from the minor hamlet of Botolph Bridge at Orton Longueville, while at Orton Waterville the pub name reflects what was once a common sight in the east of England in the Windmill.

Orwell

Found in the Domesday record of 1086 as Ordeuuelle, this name comes from Old English *ord wella* and describes the 'spring by a pointed hill'.

The hill in question shows signs of mining for the traditional building material called clunch. This is not a material in the normal sense but a wider term covering any irregular rock with a base of clay or chalk. It is used with a mortar in the building of walls.

Ouse, River

First found in 1012 as Use, later as Huse in 1244, and as the modern form for the first time in 1331, this name has been the subject of much discussion over the last century. It is generally agreed that this is a result of influences from a number of languages, originally from a Celtic tongue where *udso* would simply mean 'water'.

This river is also given the name of Wysemouth, clearly the name given to its lowest point as 'the mouth of the Ouse, and one which seems to have spread back as far as Wisbech at certain times. However, it could also have been influenced by a different name for the river between these two points, a name such as Wissey which is thought to be related to Germanic root *vis*, Old English *wase*, Old Scandinavian *veisa* and German *wiese*, all of which are variations on a 'muddy place'.

Sometimes referred to as the Great Ouse it distinguishes it from the Little Ouse, a river with identical meaning and one which was once known by the alternative Brandon Water, itself an example of back-formation from that place name.

Over

Listed as Ouer in 1060 and as Ovre in 1086, this name comes from Old English *ofer* and describes the '(place at) the ridge or slope'.

Mustill's Lane is a reminder that Jonas Mustill was living here in 1891, while Skeggs Lane was named for the 1819 holdings of John Skegg of Godmanchester. Bluntishmere Drove is named for 'Blunt's *maere* or boundary'; Gravel Bridge and Gravel Road share a corruption from *goldeg* or 'golden' and tells us a yellow flower, probably marigolds, abounded here; Langridge Fen and Langridge Drove would seem to be from *lang hrycg* or 'the long ridge', but this is a modern corruption and actually derived from *lang dic* 'the long ditch'. In 1376 Hugo White was associated with White's Bank, by 1517 William Porter was working at Porter's Farm, and Watt's Fen Farm was home to William Watts before 1787.

Locals enjoy a drink at the Admiral Vernon, named after the naval hero of 1739. Edward Vernon (1684-1757) captured the Panamanian port of Porto Bello from the Spanish with just six vessels under his command. Vernon also served several terms as a Member of Parliament, firstly representing Penryn and later Ipswich.

P

Pampisford

At the time of Domesday in 1086, when the manor was held between six different individuals, this place is recorded as Pampesuuorde. Here a Saxon personal name precedes Old English *worth* and tells us it was 'Pamp's enclosure'.

Creek's Plantation was associated with John de Crek in 1305, a man whose name probably indicates the family came from Creake in Norfolk. Brant Ditch End is derived from 'burnt ditch', this is is a lasting reminder of how it was cleared although locals always refer to it as Brandy Gin. The White Horse public house is named from the emblem representing the House of Hanover, rulers in England for some 170 years.

Papworth (Everard and St Agnes)

With records of Pappawyrthe in 1012, Papeuuorde in 1086, Anneys Papwrth in 1241, and Pappewrth Everard in 1254, this shows the basic name of these places to be from a Saxon personal name and Old English *worth* informing us these were both known as 'the enclosure of a man called Pappa'. Additions are required to distinguish between two places less than half a mile apart, these coming from the twelfth century owners named Evrard and Agnes respectively.

At Papworth St Agnes we find Nill Well, this spring started off as *cnoll* 'rounded hill' and has become corrupted to *cnyll* and hence the modern name. In the early thirteenth century the manor belonged to the Russell family, later passing to the Papworths, and from there to the Mallorys. Sir Thomas Mallory died in Papworth St Agnes in the fifteenth century, he is best known as the author of *Morte d'Arthur*, the romantic tales based on legends surrounding King Arthur, Queen Guinevere, Sir Lancelot and the Knights of the Round Table. This work takes traditional English and French writings and combines them, with a little of Mallory's own imagination, to produce the work which proved the basis for most of the writings which followed. Indeed both Tennyson's *The Idylls of the King* and *The Once and Future King* by T. H. White owe much to Mallory's work.

Parson Drove

Found as Personesdroue in 1324, this name seems to come from a combination of Middle English *persone* and Old English *drove* which describes 'the cattle road belonging to or alongside land held by a parson'.

Minor names here include Silver's Lane, home to Geoffrey Silveroun by 1345; Cannon Field was once owned by the canons of St John's Hospital, Cambridge; Diglin's Drove was associated with Thomas Diglin in 1662; and Fountain's Drove was named for being the abode of John, son of Isaac Fountaine in 1668.

The names of North Inham Field and South Inham Field show these were not farmed until the settlement was well established for these tell us they were 'the piece of land newly taken into cultivation', an extension of the available farmland. Bythorn comes from *byht hyrne* and tells of 'the nook of land in the bend of a stream'. Throckenholt is a very specific name, referring to 'the piece of timber to which the ploughshare was fastened' and would have been the wood where such was obtained.

The Butchers Arms Inn is a more common name than would be thought, for the local inn-keeper would often double as the village butcher. The Five Bells alludes to the church, although the idea of five bells in the belfry is unlikely and thus is probably heraldic which is also the most likely explanation for the Swan Inn.

The famous diarist Samuel Pepys wrote of Parson Drove in his diary of 1663. Clearly Pepys was not greatly enamoured of the village in which he stayed just two nights, September 17th and 18th. He describes this as 'a heathen place', adding this was where his horse was stolen.

Paxton (Great and Little)

Two places sharing a common origin and only a mile apart, require additions for distinction. Here the Domesday record of Pachstone shows this comes from a Saxon personal name and Old English *tun* and describing 'Paecc's farmstead'. Here the additions are self-explanatory, although today Great Paxton ironically covers less area than Little Paxton. However perhaps size was never the reason for these additions, much as 'high' is used in place names to indicate stature or importance, perhaps this is also true here.

Peakirk

Domesday lists this name as Praxemere, a name which comes from Old English *pise mere* and speaks of 'the pond where peas grow'. The modern form shows Scandinavian influence who misunderstood the name as referring to a 'church' from Old Scandinavian *kirkja*.

Peterborough

While the modern name is seen in Domesday as Burg in 1086 and as Petreburgh in 1333, there is an earlier record of Medeshamstede in the seventh century. This early record comes from a Saxon personal name and Old English *ham stede*, telling of 'the homestead of a man called Mede'. It was around this time the original monastery was built. Later the abbey was dedicated to St Peter, the dedication being added to the *burh* or 'fortification' to produce the present name. The district known as the Soke of Peterborough comes from Old English *socn* and refers specifically to 'the district under the jurisdiction of Peterborough'.

Street names here include Cowgate, which led from the butcher's quarter to the market where the meat was sold. Cumbergate was home to the woolcombers, similarly a place next the skin market. Priestgate is named for its association with Abbot Martin. Westgate has nothing to do with the compass point but is a corruption of Webstergate meaning 'the street of the weavers'.

Priestgate, Peterboroug

Pipe Lane was the location of a number of makers of clay pipes. Taverner's Street is, somewhat predictably, a place where there were numerous public houses. Narrow Street is not noticeably any narrower than other old streets. It is named for where it headed, indeed it was originally called Narrow Bridge Street.

People have also offered their names to streets here. Wellington Street remembers the solider and politician the Duke of Wellington. Gladstone Street is unlikely to be from former prime minister William Gladstone but to his brother Thomas whose political career was associated with Peterborough. Mayor's Walk is clearly associated with mayoral office. Cromwell Street recalls the political association of the county with Oliver Cromwell. Bright Street, Russell Street, Cobden Street, Montague Street, and Fane Street also have political connections, the names of members of parliament.

Hankey Street is named after Thomas Hankey, director of the Bank of England. English Street recalls Marcus English of the Freehold Land

Society and who was also a founder of English Bros the local timber merchants. Harris Street is after William Harris, also of the Freehold Land Society who owned a local grocer's business. Joseph Serjeant, butcher and member of the Freehold Land Society, gave his name to Serjeant Street. Hardware merchant and member of the Freehold Land Society William Rogers gave his name to Rogers Street, which has since been renamed Clarence Road.

The church dedication gave a name to St Leonard's Street. A name such as Monument Street refers to that erected to commemorate those who fell in battle. Landed families hereabout have given names to Fitzwilliam Street, Huntly Street and Granville Street, all of whom have too many representatives for us to have any idea if a single person was the reason for the choice of name. Allens Lane, now called Crawthorne Road, was named after a family of market gardeners, while the present name is from the Crawthorne family, here by at least the seventeenth century.

Queen Street remembers Britain's longest reigning monarch, Queen Victoria, while Jubilee Street was named to commemorate her Golden Jubilee in 1887. Stanley Road marks the achievements and work of the Stanley Recreation Council. Marne Avenue marks two decisive victories over the allies in battles at opposite ends of the First World War, at the beginning in 1914 and in the final year of 1918.

Local pubs include the Cavendish, named for the family who held the land here, better known as the dukes of Devonshire. The Exeter Arms most often refers specifically to Donald Finley, winner of the gold medal in the hurdles race at the Amsterdam Olympics of 1928, later to become Marquis of Exeter. The Gladstone Arms remembers one of nation's most influential politicians. Liberal Party leader from 1868-94, William Ewart Gladstone served as prime minister on no less than four occasions.

The Solstice, is an astronomical term referring to those two days of the year when the sun spends the longest and shortest periods in the sky and prefixed by Summer and Winter respectively. The reasons for the choice of name are unclear, however as a modern name it should be applauded for its originality.

Trees are comparatively long-lived and stand out, making them excellent markers. Thus many pubs take such names to refer to a prominent nearby tree, examples here include the Lime Tree, Cherry Tree, Elm Tree Tavern, and Walnut Tree. Although undoubtedly many tree names were chosen as the simply made for an attractive sign.

Religion may seem an odd subject for pub names in the modern era, however historically the church and the local were the two buildings

Peterborough Town Hall

where villagers would congregate, the rest of the week being spent working the land. Names here include the obvious Abbey Hotel, Angel Inn, Bell, Blue Bell Inn, Eight Bells, Six Bells, and Old Monk. The College Arms marks a connection with the church as where clergy gather and unite in a common cause. The Cross Keys Inn is ranks among the most popular of religious names, even if it is not readily obvious this symbol represents St Peter. One name which would never be associated with religion is the Fayre Spot and Goodley, which is a direct quote from a twelfth century monk of Peterborough who described the area exactly as such in his written history of the abbey.

Standing alongside the city's rowing and canoeing course, the Boathouse is a most fitting name for the local pub. The Decoy is another referring to the wetlands, used to attract waterfowl, the Ruddy Duck having similar beginnings, while the Dragonfly will make use of most still or slow-flowing waters. Other birds may refer either to the birds themselves or could have been used in coats of arms, locally we find the Golden Pheasant, Peacock, Falcon, Heron, Cock Inn, White Swan, Harrier, and the Phoenix, the latter almost always suggesting a business which had been revived just as the fabled bird said to have died in flames every five centuries only to be reborn from its own ashes.

Animals are equally as common as birds and, once again, could be either a reference to the animal or an heraldic symbol. Here we find the Bull, Dog in a Doublet, Goat, and the Durham Ox, the latter certainly a place where this huge beast was shown when touring the country, a two ton animal which cost £250 and made much more until it fell from the specially built vehicle and died from the resulting injuries. Creatures preceded by a colour are inevitably heraldic in origin, names such as the Black Horse, White Horse, Golden Lion and Blue Boar found locally. The Greyhound could be an heraldic reference to the dukes of Newcastle, or a stop for the Greyhound coach during the coaching era. The latter subject is seen in the Postilion, a pub name which began as referring to a post boy, later describing the man who rode the leading horse in a team of four pulling a carriage and also to refer to a driver of such a team; while the Coach & Horses was clearly one stop on the route.

Trades are often seen in pub names, although it is often impossible to tell why the names were chosen, either a trade associated with a landlord earlier in his life, perhaps one linked to the potential patrons, or maybe this represents the trade used as a surname. Peterborough has the Carpenters Arms, Ploughman, Three Horseshoes, Waggon and Horses, Drapers Arms, and Coalheavers Arms. No trade is more often seen in pub

Peterborough Cathedra

names than that of brewing, local examples include the Old Still and Brewery Tap. To some degree the Crab & Winkle is also an advertisement, not the modern pub grub but from the days when the 'seafood man' was a regular visitor with his basket of wares.

The Fox & Hounds advertises itself as a meeting place for the hunt; the Fenman offers hospitality to those who live and work around the area; the Kings Head shows allegiance to the Crown, although to balance that there is also the name of the Roundhead; the Rose & Crown is similarly patriotic, as indeed is the Rose Inn; the Silver Jubilee was renamed for the twenty-fifth year of the reign of Elizabeth II in 1977.

The Spring takes the name of a natural water source; the Dragon is heraldic and has probably lost a colour over the years; the George and Angel is an unusual combination, probably showing a union of names referring to the patron saint of England and to the church; the Office tells of the former use of the building; likewise so does the Old Coach House show it was a stop on the route.

The Paul Pry is the name of a play written by John Poole. First produced in 1825, the eponymous character is forever interfering in the lives of others. The play proved extremely popular and toured the land for some time. Perhaps the pub sign featuring a man listening at a door marked 'Private' is a copy of the poster used to advertise the play at the local theatre.

People are often chosen for pub names, either national heroes or local figures. The Admiral Wells, which has genuine claims as the nation's lowest pub above sea level, is named after the family who were Kent shipbuilders from the seventeenth century. They came to Cambridgeshire when William Wells inherited the estate from his wife's family around 1760. A successful naval career came to a premature end when he died aged 51 in 1811 having commanded eight vessels over a twenty-three year

Tudor House, Peterborough

period. He was afforded the honour of pallbearer at Lord Nelson's funeral in 1805. The Crown & Anchor features the badge of the lord high admiral, and also features on the arm of the Royal Navy's petty officers, and is a name favoured by many retired seaman.

John Clare (1793-1864) was a poet whose works all had a rural theme. Before his name was used on the sign outside the pub he had had a chequered life, as herd-boy, soldier, a failed farmer, and even as a vagrant. Such a lifestyle undoubtedly resulted in his insanity at the age of 44.

The Sibson Inn takes its name from the farm of this name which had occupied this site since the late seventeenth century. The Northfield is a second which takes a local name, itself one which is self-explanatory. The Posh Pub suggests one of superior quality, while also being the nickname of the local football club, Peterborough United. With the many links to flight around this part of England, Whittle Way is named to remember Sir Frank Whittle, inventor of the jet engine.

The Old Locomotive is easily seen as a link to the nearby railway. The Hand and Heart is a reference to the once common symbol of two hands holding a single heart, representing friendship it suggests a warm welcome is to be found within. A Volunteer was one who was not a member of the regular army but those who offered their services and particularly during the Napoleonic wars, the Swiss Cottage describes the building, and the Straw Bear is the central image of an annual festival held on the Tuesday after Plough Monday whose origins are shrouded in mystery.

Pidley

Here is 'Pyda's woodland clearing', where the Saxon personal name is followed by Old English *leah*. The name is recorded as Pydele in 1228, the earliest known listing of this name.

Here the local pub goes under the odd name of the Mad Cat, which is undoubtedly unique even if the etymology is not. Many pub names are chosen for the simple imagery for three reasons: easily recognised, easy to understand, and easy to reproduce and therefore cheap. The third reason does have its pitfalls, for paying a local to produce a sign is not always the best idea. An example is found here, for the innkeeper requested an image of a White Lion, which locals said looked more like a Mad Cat. The name stuck and was later made official.

Plantwater Drain

Found as Plantecrofte in 1320, Idenhea Plant in 1436, Plant's were in 1438, and Plantinwater in 1636, there are two distinct names for this watercourse. In 1270 there is a record at Wisbech of "the sewer called Idenhea being in bredth 32 foote", Ide being an unexplained river name found elsewhere. The alternative comes from Old English *plante* meaning 'a plant shoot' and is derived from a word meaning 'spreading', thus perhaps there was once a plant here which was spreading to cover the general area.

Preceptory

This place was named after the Preceptory of the Knights of the Hospital of Jerusalem, land granted to the order by King John in 1199.

Prickwillow

What appears an unusual name turns out to be quite descriptive when the name is defined. First seen in a document of 1251, recorded as Prickewylev, this name comes from Old English *pricca wilig* and describes 'the willow tree from which skewers and goads are made'.

Much of this area lies below sea level, thus it was necessary to pump the water from here to keep the fertile land from becoming waterlogged. To achieve this a series of engines were installed. First came the Side Lever Steam Engine in 1831, later replaced by the Beam Steam Engine in 1880, thereafter the diesel powered Mirless Bickerton and Day Diesel Engine in 1924, and finally an automated electric system in 1970.

Q

Quy Water

An unusual name which comes from the Old English *cu eg*, telling us it was 'the drier ground in a marsh where cows are pastured'. While the land name is now lost it was transferred to the wetland and continues to this day.

R

Rampton

This name is recorded in Domesday as Rantone, a name derived from Old English *ramm tun* or 'the farmstead where rams are kept'.

Minor names here include Pauley's Drove, the 'drovers' route associated with William Pawley' who was here by 1840. Giant's Grave is named after a large mound found near Giants Hill, which has taken the name of this man-made feature.

Rampton is a rarity for it has one of the very few English churches with a thatched roof. There is also an annual summer fete held on the village green. A pantomime is performed after which every villager over the age of 55 is given a free, and apparently sumptuous, dinner.

Ramsey

The earliest known record of this name is from around 1000 as Hramesege, which shows this comes from Old English *hramsa eg* and describes 'the dry ground in a marsh where wild garlic grows'. When comparing this with the previous entry it is clear how important it is to find as many early forms as possible, for here it would have been easy to see the first element as *ramm* or 'male sheep'.

The White Lion is a pub name with an heraldic reference to Edward IV, the dukes of Norfolk, or the earls of March. There can be no doubt the Angel is another showing the close relationship between the pub and the church within the community, similarly the Cross Keys is representative of St Peter although this is not the dedication of any church here. The George at Ramsey takes its name from King George's Field, itself a memorial to King George V. The Jolly Sailor takes a common name, probably a former occupation of a landlord, and adds a message suggesting this is a place of great contentment. The Lion is heraldic, the Railway built to welcome travellers when that new form of transport arrived in Ramsey, and the Three Horseshoes from an earlier age when the horse was the sole mode of power.

Raveley (Great and Little)

Separated by less than a mile, these two place names share a common origin and are recorded as Raeflea in 1060. Here the additions are clear, while the basic name is from Old English *hraefn leah* and describes 'the woodland clearing where ravens are seen'.

Reach

Domesday records this name as Reche, which comes from Old English *rec* and describes the '(place at) the raised strip of land'. Here that raised land is Devil's Dyke, an earthwork which archaeologists have shown is of post-Roman origins. A third name comes from the same feature, the public house known as the Dykes End.

Here the fen waterway system made Reach an important economic centre, with goods unloaded at the wharf of hythe to the Saxons. However there remains an even earlier waterway, a Roman canal, the Reach Lode, still navigable in the twenty-first century.

Redmere

This name is found as Redemere in 1251, Rodemere in 1298, and Redmore in 1825. This comes from Old English *reed mere* and describes 'the pool where reeds are obtained'.

Rhee, River

A name which is quite common and one which combines Old English *ea* 'river' and Middle English *atter* 'at the', where the end of the first word of *atter ea* has been confused with being part of the second element.

Ripton (Abbots and Kings)

Listed as Riptone in 960 and as Riptune in 1086, this name comes from Old English *rip tun* and refers to this as 'the farmstead by a strip of land'. The additions here show the respective place were held by the Abbot of Ramsey and the crown respectively.

Running Ditch

These waters flow, via the North Ditch, into the Cam. The original name was the Marditch meaning the 'boundary ditch' and the modern version either means exactly the same, 'running along the boundary' or perhaps 'running water'.

S

St Ives

This place is name for the relics of St Ivo, found here in the tenth century. This is the reason this place was recorded as Sancto Ivo de Slepe in 1110. Here the earlier name can be seen as Slepe, itself from Old English *slaep* meaning 'slippery place'.

One local pub is the Seven Wives, where the sign depicts the image of the riddle which asks:

> *"As I was going to St Ives,*
> *I met a man with seven wives,*
> *Each wife had seven sacks,*
> *Each sack had seven cats,*
> *Each cat had seven kits,*
> *Kits, cats, sacks, and wives,*
> *How many were going to St Ives?"*

The Aviator shows how the many airfields used by the forces during the Second World War were situated to the east of England; the Black Bull is heraldic; the Floods Tavern a reminder of the chances of floods in the fens; the Old Ferry Boat Inn is another reminder of the water courses here; the Greyhound symbolises the dukes of Newcastle; the Haywain takes the name of the famous painting by John Constable; Nelsons Head commemorates the nation's greatest hero; the Oliver Cromwell remembers the man whose life and family came from around here; the Pike & Eel were caught regularly, in earlier times important food items; the Robin Hood invariably depicts the hero of Sherwood Forest, but began life as the image of a Forester; the Unicorn symbolises Scotland; the White Hart was once the generic name for a public house, much as the 'hoover' is used for a vacuum cleaner today.

St Ives Bridge is one of only five in the country to have a chapel as part of its construction. Pay close attention to the arches here and it is clear the bridge has been built at two different times for the two southern arches are rounded, not gothic. The bridge was repaired after being blown up by Oliver Cromwell's men to prevent the king and his followers making their way through here to reach London.

St Neots

Another saint, this time the place is recorded as S'Neod in the twelfth century. This was named from St Neot, whose relics were brought here from Cornwall in the tenth century.

Street names in St Neots do reflect the history of the town. Church Street was named for the dedication of the church to St Mary, with the street formerly known as Saynt Maristrete. Other streets have only comparatively recent taken the name by which they are known today. Brook Street may well have been the local name but it was not adopted officially until as late as 1878. The origin of South Street needs no explanation, although previously it was known as Bell Lane after the Bell Inn. Market Square has always been known for its market, although previously it was referred to as Market Place, and before that Market Street. High Street is, as with most streets of this name, an indication it was the most important in the town.

Cemetery Lane has had more names than most. In the seventeenth century it was Duck Lane, in the eighteenth century Little Bridge Street, by 1848 Brick Kiln Lane and only by its modern name after the consecrated ground was established here in 1879. It is also noted that regular churchgoers were most vociferous in their protest of the appalling idea of non-conformists being given a burial in consecrated ground.

Windmill Row was developed by James Tristham, who set up home here after he retired as a miller, hence the name. Cambridge Street and Huntingdon Street were named after the two major towns in the area. New Street, earlier known as New Lane, was first seen as Neystrete in 1505, the first known mention which still makes it over five centuries old and not particularly 'new'.

Bedford Street is a name clearly after the county town of Bedfordshire. However earlier it was known as John Nutters Lane, which was then abbreviated to Nutters Lane. It was given its modern name by the Local Board in 1878, a deliberate change for they objected to the idea suggested by the then current name, even though they almost certainly would have been aware it was named after John Nutter.

Russell Street remembers Lord John Russell, the great radical and parliamentarian reformer who represented the Huntingdonshire Divisions from about 1820. Often said to have been named after the Lord John Russell public house, this is not possible as the road was known as such well before 1870 and the pub was known as The Boot until that year.

Loves Farm remembers Adam Love, whose tombstone can still be seen in the churchyard with an inscription which reads:

Why wonder we that man no more
Is by affection led
When this sad stone declares to all
Alas, that Love is dead
Why what the history of the past
Is cruelty and pride
When this same monument records
That Love with Adam died.

Pubs here include the Hyde Park which, while possibly inspired by the famous London park, it is more likely to be a local name referring to the ancient measurement of land; the Barley Mow points to the stack of barley, recently harvested and ready for the brewery; the Bell shows the traditional link between the pub and the church, as does the Priory; heraldic signs, not always of known origin, include the Bulls Head, the Falcon, the Old Falcon, Spread Eagle Inn, Wheatsheaf, Woolpack; the Globe may be heraldic, although it was also used as a very simple image which

Pig n Falcon, St Neots

also suggested it was open to all; trades are represented by the Millers Arms, the Plough, and the River Mill Tavern.

Others include the Wrestlers, showing a venue for this ancient sport; similarly the Hare and Hounds shows a meeting place for the hunt; the Coneygeare tells us there was a rabbit warren here, probably an indication that this food animal was farmed here. While the New Inn is of obvious origin, note many are anything but 'new' and thus should be seen as 'newer'; likewise the name of Ye Olde Sun is somewhat misleading for while it may indeed be older than another named the sun, it cannot be its original name for this is actually an American idea and only came to Britain around the end of the Victorian era.

One of St Neots most famous residents was one of the most notorious men in British political history and a name known to every trivia enthusiast. On 11th May 1812 John Bellingham entered the lobby at the Houses of Parliament and shot the serving prime minister Spencer Percival through the heart. Bellingham was having desperate money problems and had hoped to receive a generous compensation award after being unfairly imprisoned in Russia. A week later on 18th May he had been found guilty and was hanged. Ironically many pitied the widow Bellingham and her four children and donations brought a sum reputed to be ten times that they could ever have hoped to receive in the form of compensation.

Sapley

Documented as Sappele in 1227, here is a name derived from Old English *saeppe leah* which describes 'the woodland clearing by the fir trees'.

The local pub is the Longbow, a very English weapon and a very English pub name. A weapon which has become associated with the decisive victories by the English over the French at Crecy (1346), Poitiers (1356) and Agincourt (1415). However the weapon has been invented and re-invented by many cultures over the years, standards for the design in the wars against the French were very different from what was first written down by the Victorians.

Sawston

Recorded as Salsingetune in 970 and as Salsiton in 1086, this name comes from a Saxon personal name and Old English *inga tun* and tells us it was 'the farmstead of the family or followers of a man called Salse'.

Here we find Borough Grove and Borough Mill, both named from the family of William de Burgo who were here by 1236. Dernford Farm and Dernford Mill share an origin of 'the hidden ford', the mill probably came first for this is recorded as early as 956. Huckeridge Hill gets its name from 'the cross by the hill'; Deal Grove is from *dael* 'a share, a plot'; and Huntington's Farm was worked by the family of Ralph de Hintingdon in 1300.

Royalist and patriotic support is shown in the names of the Kings Head and Queens Head. Less obvious is the White Lion, an heraldic reference to Edward IV, the earls of March, and the Duke of Norfolk. The Greyhound is probably also an heraldic image representative of the dukes of Newcastle. The Black Bull is a common name, although most often not heraldic but simply a rural image, as is the Woolpack a reference to the large bales of wool, the basic measure when sold on to cloth manufacturers.

There is evidence of a Bronze Age settlement dating from five thousand years ago. This would have been the same people connected with the hill figures discovered on part of the Gog-Magog Hills, for here is the only place where such would be visible unless airborne.

Sawston Hall is a Tudor manor house dating from the sixteenth century. It was held by the same family, the Huddlestons, until the 1980s. Early in its history the hall provided a bed for Mary Tudor, soon to be Mary I and also referred to as Bloody Mary. She was on the run, trying to evade imprisonment by the Duke of Northumberland. The next morning she escaped disguised as a dairy maid while close behind were the duke's soldiers who, learning of Mary's escape, punished the family by setting fire to the medieval manor and destroying it.

Sawtry

A name which indicates just how far inland the sea could influence in the flat fenland of eastern England. Here the name comes from Old English *salt rith* and describes 'the salty stream'. This name is found as Saltreiam in a document dated 974.

The Bell Inn has a sign showing a simple and easily recognised image, most often also telling of a link to the church. Greystones must be a local name, although we should not take the first element literally as a colour but understand this is an old place name telling us it was 'a boundary stone'. If the use of 'grey' to mean 'boundary' seems unusual, remember we still refer to matters open to question as a 'grey area'.

Shelford (Great and Little)

Records of the basic name begin with Scelford in 1050 and as Escelforde in 1086, these two places are only a mile apart and thus require these additions, which need no explanation. This name comes from Old English *sceldu ford* which tells us it was 'the shallow ford'.

Local names include Nine Wells, of obvious meaning although there do not appear to be as many here today. De Freville Farm is named after the family of Richard de Frevill, who were certainly here by 1275. In 1355 John de Grendon was living at Granham's Manor Farm.

At Little Shelford we find the Navigator, a pub name which refers to the 'navvies', those men who excavated the nearby 'navigation' or canal. Great Shelford has the Plough, a name which suggests a rural location; the Square and Compasses features images of the most basic tools used by carpenters, joiners and masons; while the Railway Tavern was built to offer refreshment to travellers when the new mode of transport first came through here.

Shepreth

Domesday's record of Esceprid shows this name is from Old English *sceap rith* or 'the stream frequented by sheep'.

Huckles Lane was home to Adam and Alan Huckyl in 1279; Tyrell's Hall remembers Edward Terell in 1427 and Thomas Tyrell in 1446; Thomas Docura was living at Docuraies Manor by 1552; and John Wimbish gave his name to Wimbish Manor, where he could be found in 1422. The exception here is Brimble Hill for it is not a family name but derived from *bremel hyll* 'the hill overgrown by brambles'.

Shingay

Listed as Sceningeie, Sceneheia and Scelgei in 1086, Sebegaia in 1087, Sungheye in 1280, Synghai in 1513, and Shyngey in 1571, there are no shortage of records for this place name. Here the Saxon personal name is followed by Old English *inga eg* and describes 'the low lying land of the family or followers of Scene'. This personal name is derived from *sciene*, a root of 'scene' and meaning 'beautiful'.

Shire Drain, The

A part of the Old South Eau which is named, not surprisingly, as it forms the traditional county boundary between Tydd St Giles in Cambridgeshire and Tydd St Mary in Lincolnshire.

Sibson

Found as Sibestune in 1086, this name combines an Old Scandinavian personal name and Old English *tun* to tell us this was 'Sibbi's farmstead'.

Six Mile Bottom

A very modern name, at least when compared to the vast majority of place names in this book, and for once we know exactly when it was named for such is reported in a document dated 1801. It took the existing Old English *botm* or 'valley' and added the distance from here to Newmarket.

Snailwell

Records of this name include Sneillewelle in 1050 and as Snelleuuelle in 1086. Here, from Old English *snaegl wella*, is a name which tells us it was 'the stream infested with snails'.

The farthest part of a parish would often be given a name which suggested it might as well be in another part of the world it was so far to go to work. Such a remoteness name is given to the extreme south of the parish here, the region known as Philadelphia which we must assume was in the news when this name was coined.

Soham

As Saegham in 1000 and as Saham in 1086, this is derived from Old English *saege ham* or 'the homestead by the swampy pool'.

Street names here include two named from former inns, Cherrytree Lane and Fountain Lane. Pratt Street was home to the family of Mabilla and Thomas Prat some time before 1312, with Staples's Lane remembering the family of Edward Staples who certainly were here by 1768. Vaxen Lane is a corruption of 'backs and ends', referring to the housing built here.

It is easy to see how Barchem Farm was "where birch trees grow', while Old English *beorh eg* 'the hill island' has given rise to Barway, Barway Fen and Barraway Siding. Old English *hassuc* meaning 'coarse grass' gave names to The Hasse, Great Hasse Farm, Little Hasse Farm, and Hasse Drove, while the name of No Ditch Field started off as 'new ditch'.

People who have left their mark include John Deye, who was at Day's Farm by 1404; Robert Hicks was associated with Hick's Drove by 1840; John Hogge was living as Hodge's Hill by 1353; Elizabeth Key was linked to Key's Croft in 1840; Leonard's Farm was home to George Leonard by 1840; Newman's Pond was linked to Robert Newman before 1370; and the family of Jeremy Slack gave his name to Slack's Hill some time before 1680.

Public houses here include the most common name in the country, once having over six hundred examples in England the Red Lion most often represents Scotland. Showing a former landlord or owner had some connection with the sea is the Ship, similarly the Carpenters Arms would originally have displayed images of the tools of one of the oldest of trades, the Fountain is an heraldic sign representative of the Master Mariners or the Plumbers' Company, and the Cherry Tree would have originally referred to a nearby tree.

This place has been inhabited for a very long time. No less than two late Bronze Age hoards containing swords and spearheads were found, while a gold torc was unearthed in 1938. From at least this early era, and probably much earlier, comes a wooden trackway across the fenland. This has only been traced for some eight or nine hundred yards, yet must surely have been of much greater length as indeed are those across the Somerset levels. Wooden piles driven deep into the mud and peat of the fens supported flat planks to provide means of crossing the fens on foot.

Much of Soham may well have been erased from the face of the earth had it not been for the bravery of four railway workers on the 2nd June 1944. A train carrying munitions was necessarily travelling very slowly through the town. Probably a result of a stray spark from the funnel of the steam engine, the leading waggon of the heavy train was found to be on fire and certain to explode. With the help of signalman Frank Bridges and guard Herbert Clarke, Benjamin Gimbert and James Nightfall (driver and fireman respectively) uncoupled the engine and the now burning lead waggon and drove it away from the rest of the train and the town. The explosion did cause a lot of damage to property and took the lives of both Jim Nightfall and Frank Bridges, while Ben Gimbert was hospitalised for seven weeks. These men were awarded the George Cross, the highest civilian award for bravery.

Somersham

Without records such as Summeresham in 1000 and Sumersham in 1086, we might have thought the first element represented the warmest season. However it seems this is a Saxon personal name which, when suffixed by Old English *ham*, refers to 'Sumor or Sunmaer's homestead'.

The Windmill public house marks the position of a former windmill.

Southoe

A name from Old English *suth hoh* and which describes 'the southern hill spur', this is recorded as Sutham in 1086 and as Sudho in 1186.

The Three Horseshoes is a common name referring to the service provided by the nearby blacksmith, indeed the name should be seen as a question and thus offering to provide the fourth shoe for the traveller's horse.

Southorpe

The Domesday record of Sudtorp shows this is from Old Scandinavian *suthr thorp* and refers to this as 'the southern outlying farmstead'. The name also points out this was an overspill settlement, one originally nothing more than a seasonal group of huts, fields and pastures providing food for a growing population to the north. Over time the settlement grew eventually becoming independent.

Spaldwick

A name which is found as Spalduice in 1086, this comes from Old English *spald wic* and describes 'the specialised farm by the trickling stream'.

The George of Spaldwick is an old coaching inn opened in 1679. Most often this refers to the kings of England, members of the House of Hanover, who ruled England from 1714 to 1830. Yet the inn pre-dates the reigns of the four Georges, hence this is either not the original name or a reference to a different George, most likely St George, the patron saint of England.

Stapleford

Here is 'the ford marked by posts' from Old English *stapol ford* and found in documents dated 956 and 1086 as Stapelforda and Stapelforde, respectively.

Local place names of note cover several eras. The oldest Saxon names are seen in Vandlebury or 'Waendel's fortification', and Wormwood Hill is a reference to a *wyrm* or 'dragon', a fabled monster said to be living in a tumulus here. Other burial mounds have the names of The Loaves and The Twopenny Loaves, clearly a reference to their size and shape. There is also Telegraph Clump, the site of an old signalling station.

One local is the Longbow, a pub name referring to the weapon which gave the English armies a massive advantage in their battles with the French from the fourteenth century. There is also the Tree, a common source of names for pubs as they are large and long-lived and serve as markers.

Stetchworth
Seen as Steuicheswrthe in 1050 and Stiuicesuuorde in 1086, this is either from Old English *styfic worth* and 'the enclosure among the tree stumps' or the first element is a personal name and therefore 'Styfic's enclosure'.

Kidney Plantation is named for its distinctive shape, Two Captains refers to the field containing two burial mounds, while Two Hills is the name given to the neighbouring field with a double rise.

Stibbington
Domesday's listing of Stebintune shows this name is probably derived from a Saxon personal name and Old English *ing tun* which tells us it was 'the farmstead associated with a man called Stybba'. However this may represent *stybbing tun* and refer to 'the farmstead of or marked by the tree stumps'.

Stilton
The real home of the cheese which was developed here and sold in Leicestershire, the name is derived from Old English *stigel tun* which tells us it was 'the farmstead at a stile'. The name is recorded in Domesday as Stichiltone.

Doubtless they serve the eponymous cheese with the ploughman's lunch at the Stilton Cheese Inn, and probably also the Bell Inn, itself derived from the close association between pub and church, and the Talbot Inn, the breed of dog which was the forerunner of the foxhound.

The cheese itself must have had an original recipe and a creator. Its popularity was spread after being tasted at the coaching inns, evidence exists in the original hand of Daniel Defoe (author of *Robinson Crusoe*), who expressed his liking for the cheese in 1722. Traditionally the cheese was made by the housekeeper of Quenby Hall, Hungarton, near Melton Mowbray in Leicestershire and brought here to add to the menus of the coaching inns via her brother-in-law. Interestingly legislation has since been passed banning the manufacture of stilton cheese anywhere but the traditional sites in Derbyshire, Leicestershire and Nottinghamshire meaning it is now illegal to make stilton cheese in Stilton.

Stonely
Not found until 1280 when it appears as Stanlegh, this comes from Old English *stan leah* and describes 'the stony woodland clearing'.

Stow cum Quy
One of the most common elements in place names is here found with one of the most unusual. Recorded as Stoua in 1086, Coiea in 1086, and Stowe cum Quey in 1316, this comes from Old English *stow* a word referring to either 'the assembly place' although perhaps 'holy place' should not be ruled out. The addition was, as evidenced by Domesday, a separate settlement with a name from Old English *cu eg* or 'cow island'. Joining the two is Latin *cum* meaning 'with' and an element which can only have originated through the written record.

Here we find Collier's Lane, named after Trignell Collyer who was here before the record of 1840, and D'Engayne's Farm, remembering the family of William Dengayne who were here by 1279.

The locals enjoy a glass of their favourite tipple at the White Swan, a fairly modern name for such places were always simply the 'Swan' as all known swans were white until the discovery of Australia and its black swan. Invariably the sign is heraldic, found in the arms of the Vintners' Company, the Poulters' Company, the Musicians' Company, and of the earls of Essex and King Edward III.

The Wheatsheaf is a pub name derived from either the Worshipful Company of Bakers or the Brewers Company, as early innkeepers would have provided a second service to the community, most often as a butcher or baker. While this may seem strange today, remember passing trade was not enough to maintain a living and there was a limit to the amount of ale which a small community could consume or afford to buy! The Prince

Albert remembers Francis Albert Augustus Charles Emmanuel, son of Ernest I, Duke of Saxe-Coburg-Gotha and consort of Queen Victoria.

Streetly End

Listed in Domesday as Stradleia, this name is from Old English *straet leah* which tells us it was 'the woodland clearing by the Roman road'. The addition is a modern development, probably thought to refer to the 'end' of the street when this was certainly not the case.

Stretham

A name which can still be seen as coming from Old English *straet ham* and referring to 'the homestead by the Roman road'. The name is found as Stratham in 970 and as Stradham in the Domesday record of 1086, when it was a possession of the Abbot of Ely.

Elford Close takes its name from *eald ford* 'the old ford' where the Akeman Street crossed the River Ouse. Lazier Fen takes its name from *laes* meaning 'pasture', while Snott's Common is from *snote* or 'snout' and a description of the shape of this piece of land.

Animals are a popular subject for a pub sign, easily recognised and make for an attractive sign. Here the nearby River Ouse was probably the inspiration for choosing our most famous aquatic mammal, *Lutra lutra* is here depicted on the sign of the Lazy Otter. The Red Lion is the most common pub name in the land. Most often attributed to symbolise Scotland, it was first seen in England when representing John of Gaunt, the most powerful man in England during the fourteenth century and whose bedroom antics could be said to have resulted in the Wars of the Roses. Indeed the illegitimate family he sired early in his life went on to form an unbroken line of Scots monarchs from 1603 and thereafter, when James VI of Scotland acceded to the English throne as James I, his ancestors sat on the English throne.

In 1952 workers uncovered a fossil of 130 million year old pliosaur from the Jurassic period. While the teeth of this animal are a common fossil full skeletons are extremely rare.

Stukeley (Great and Little)

Found as Stivecle in 1086, these places share a common origin in Old English *styfic leah* and describe 'the woodland clearing with tree stumps'.

The additions need no explanation except that they are necessary as these places are less than a mile apart.

The Three Horseshoes was a sign indicating the pub had a blacksmith, an advertisement for the metalworker who would re-shoe the clients' horse. Indeed the name should be regarded as a question, hence one shoe less than the four on a horse.

Stuntney

Domesday records this name as Stuntenei, a name from Old English *stunt eg* which tells us it was 'the steep place at the dry ground in a marsh'.

Hatch's Farm was home to the family of John Hatch by 1802, while Skirts Row described a long row of trees marking the edge of the fen.

Sutton

One of the most common place names in the land, the only surprise here is there is no addition to distinguish it from others. The name comes from Old English *suth tun* and describes 'the southern farmstead', clearly named from a settlement to the north of here. The name is found in Domesday as Sudtone. One local name compliments this, although at first glance it is difficult to see The Beesons coming from *bi eastan tun*, it does describe the '(place) by the eastern farmstead'.

As a place name Brangehill Drove began life as describing 'the corner of land of the family or followers of Beorna'. Coming from the later Middle English *galle*, the name of Gault Bridge describes itself as being on 'the marshy ground'. Jolly Banker's Bridge took its name from the inn of that name here. Sun Doles is derived from *suthan dole* 'the southern allocations of land'.

People have left their mark here too: Beddingham's Farm was worked by Richard Bedyngham in 1461; Sarah Blaby was associated with Blaby's Drove in 1692; Chaffey's Farm remembers William Chaffey, here in 1840; Charter's Farm is named after the family of William Charter, who were here by 1811; Feary's Farm is a reminder of Stephen Feary, here by 1773; Robinson's Farm was associated with John Robinson by 1768; Tubb's Farm was home to the family of William Tubb by 1654; and William Watte was near what is now Watt's Drove some time before 1369.

Swaffham (Bulbeck and Prior)

Only a mile separates these places where the additions refer to possession by the de Bolbech family and the Abbot of Ely, respectively. The basic name is of Old English origins in *Swaefe ham* and describing 'the homestead of the Swabians', a Germanic people. Records of these places include Suafham in 1050, Swafham Bolebek in 1218 and as Swafham Prior in 1261.

Swaffham Bulbeck has minor names such as Crow Hill Plantation, nothing to do with birds but comes from Old English *creowel* meaning 'fork', a description of some feature they saw in the landscape. Individuals who have left their mark include Benjamin Ashman, who was at Ashman's Farm by 1722, Thomas de Burgh, associated with Burgh Hall in 1327, and Sarra Sorel, who gave a name to Sorrel Farm some time after 1318. The pub here is the Black Horse, a name which is used to symbolise several things including a well-known bank, goldsmiths, the Dragoon Guards, and many, many more.

At Swaffham Prior we find Lord's Ground Farm, named after Adam le Lord who was here in 1280. Delver End and Delver Bridge share a name from *delf ende* 'that end of the parish with diggings', possibly a quarry. The local name of Reach is from Old English *raec* meaning 'strip, stripe', a topographical feature and most likely a ploughed length, although it could also be *rake* and telling of 'a steep, narrow path'. Both Barston Bridge and Barston Drove are derived from *baest tun* and speak of 'the farmstead of the lime trees'. The Red Lion is the most common pub name in the land, most often symbolising Scotland.

Swavesey

Listed in Domesday as Suauesye, this name comes from a Saxon personal name and Old English *hyth* which together describe 'the landing place of a man named Swaef'. This is probably a nickname meaning 'the Swabian'.

Buckingway House was built on the place which derived its name from one of two possible origins. Either this is 'Bucc's track', or possibly this name tells of 'the track of the people of Boxworth'.

The White Horse Inn undoubtedly refers to the heraldic image associated with the House of Hanover. The Trinity Foot public house takes the name from the chairman of the brewery which once owned this establishment, he being Master of Trinity College Foot Beagles while at Cambridge University.

T

Tadlow

Here is a Saxon personal name preceding Old English *hlaw* and telling us of 'Tada's tumulus'. The name is found as Tadeslaue in 1080 and as Tadelai in 1086.

Locally we find Pincote Barn, a Saxon personal name and Old English *cote* and thus 'the cottages of a man called Pin'. The farthest corner of the parish was often given an ironic name, an exaggeration of its distance from the centre of the place and categorized as a remoteness name, the example here being New England Farm.

Teversham

Found in Domesday as Teuersham, this name comes from Old English *tiefrere ham* which describes this as 'the homestead of the painter or sorcerer'. However it is also possible this first element is used as a personal name.

In 1386 the family of John Aleyn were working the land here, in the area now known as Allen's Farm. The Rose & Crown shows the landlord was a patriot and a supporter of the monarchy.

Thetford

A name from Old English *theod ford* which describes 'the public ford', probably saying it was toll free. These names are recorded as Thiutforda in 972 and Liteltedford in 1086, showing there are actually two places, with the other from Old English *lytel* and of obvious meaning.

At Little Thetford we find Watson's Lane, recalling the Watson family who were here by 1617, while Gold's Mere is of even earlier derivation, Richard Golde is the first recorded representative of this family and he was here by 1285. The Fish & Duck Inn points to its location near the confluence of the Great Ouse and the Cam.

Thorney

A name found as Thornige in 960 and as Torny in the Domesday record of 1086, this is a name of Old English origin from *thorn eg* and describes 'the thorn tree island'. The Thorney River, a tributary of the Nene, takes its name from the place.

Thorney village sign

Minor names here include Gold Dike, a misleading name for it simply describes 'the bounds of the Abbot of Thorney'. Singlesole Farm features an Old German personal name with *holt* and tells us it was 'Singhulph's woodland'. The name of Wryde Croft comes from Old English *wride* referring to the 'twisting stream'. French Drove can be dated back to when a colony of French peasant refugees were living here between 1653 and 1721.

The local pub is the Black Hart which, until we see it written, brings to mind the image of a rather unsavoury character. However the true origin is the deer, here the colour indicating it is an heraldic reference.

Thorney Abbey

In the seventeenth century a number of Walloon Protestant refugees settled here from the Flanders region in northern France. The topography of the two regions is very similar and these settlers were experts in draining fenland. On the outskirts of the village was the windmill, a large construction which had six sails and the same number of floors.

Thornhaugh

With the earliest known record as Thornhawe in 1189, we can see this is from Old English *thorn haga* and refers to 'the thorn tree enclosure'.

Thriplow

A name where a Saxon personal name is suffixed by Old English *hlaw* and describes 'Tryypa's tumulus'. This name appears as Tripelan and Trepeslau in 1050 and 1086 respectively.

Bacon's Farm was worked by Thomas Bacun by 1316, while Nicholas de Barenton was at Barrington's Manor Farm by 1250. St John's College Farm was left in the will of Dr Humphrey Gower in 1711 to his successors, the Masters of St John's College, Cambridge. The name of Great Nine Wells, first seen in 1825, requires no explanation, other than to say the addition of 'Great' distinguishes this from Little Nine Wells in Whittlesford and Nine Wells in Great Shelford.

Tilbrook

Listed in Domesday as Tilebroc, this name probably comes from 'Tila's brook' and where a Saxon personal name is followed by Old English *broc*.

The White Horse is a pub name coming from the heraldic image of the royal House of Hanover.

Toft

Old Scandinavian *toft* is a word describing 'a curtilage or homestead', the name being recorded as Tofth in Domesday.

Miller's Road is named after the Reverend George Miller, who could be found in the local church by 1840.

Toseland

A name of Old Scandinavian origin featuring a personal name and *lundr*, which means this was 'Toli's woodland grove'. The name is found as Toleslund in 1086.

Trumpington

Found as Trumpintune in 1050 and as Trumpintone in 1086, this combines a Saxon personal name and Old English *ing tun* to tell us it was 'the farmstead associated with a man called Truma'.

Kneighton is an unusual modern form of Old English *cyne tun* or 'the royal manor', most often seen simply as 'Knighton'. Anstey Hall is after Christopher Anstey, rector of Brinkley who held land here before his death in 1751.

One local is the Green Man, a common name which is often depicted as a Robin Hood figure. This is not the legendary hero, nor is it one of his Merry Men, but a woodsman wearing the green in which this band of outlaws are invariably depicted. Despite the liking for animals on pub signs, The Unicorn is a splendid image of a white horse with a single long horn and a fabled creature which was used in heraldry to represent Scotland, the Worshipful Company of Wax Chandlers, the Worshipful Company of Goldsmiths, and Worshipful Company of Apothecaries. The Coach and Horses shows a stop on the nationwide coaching routes, while the horse carried the huntsman from the Tally Ho Inn, the name featuring the cry that went up when their prey was spotted.

Trumpington has two small claims to fame. In Geoffrey Chaucer's *Canterbury Tales*, the village is the setting for *The Reeve's Tale*. The local church contains a monumental brass to Sir Roger de Trumpington, a man who fought in the crusades and who died here in 1289. While the man himself is not particularly outstanding, his brass monument has only one older surviving example.

Tydd St Giles

The Domesday record of Tid points to this coming from Old English *tydd* which tells us it was the '(place of) the shrubs or brushwood'. The addition refers to the dedication of the church, necessary to distinguish this from another Tydd in neighbouring Lincolnshire.

Bee's Lane takes its name from William le Be, here in 1240; Black Lane is after William Blac, here in 1221; and Carveley's Lane was associated with Robert Calverley in 1671. The house named Australia was built by John Morton. Born in 1840 he saved to emigrate with his friend, but was let down at the last minute and Morton decided to remain in England rather than start a new life on the other side of the world where he knew nobody. Instead he worked and eventually built the house here, which he named Australia to mark dreams never realised.

Blowhead Field takes its name from Old English *blaw heafod* 'the cold headland'; a name which tells us it was a 'summer pasture' is today marked on the map as Summer Leisure Field; John Cooper was at Cooper's Farm by 1840; his neighbour in that year was Richard Oldroyd at Oldroyd's Farm; Crane Cottage was home to William Crane in 1802; and Mark Kenny was living at Kenny House in 1830.

It must be said the name of the Crown & Mitre is most unexpected, although the imagery is clear. This represents the monarchy and the church, although there must be something else in this message, for historically the two factions were forever at odds. Unfortunately the original message is unknown.

U

Ufford

From a Saxon personal name together with Old English *worth*, this name speaks of 'Uffa's enclosure'. The name is recorded as Uffawyrtha in 948.

Upware

The name of Upware has two elements, the first is self-explanatory while the second is from Old English *waer* and speaking of 'the higher weir'.

The local pub may well qualify as the longest pub name in the land and tells its own story, albeit in part inaccurately, as the Five Miles From Anywhere No Hurry Inn.

Upwell

Found as Wellan in 963 and as Upwell in a document dated 1221, this name describes the '(place) higher upstream'. Here is a name from Old English *upp wella*.

Local names include Birdbeck Field, derived from Old English *budda bece* and telling us it was 'the stream frequented by dung beetles'. Shrewsness Green may be a warning it was somewhere to avoid for the name literally means 'the villain's headland', however the majority of such names refer to this as land taken by another in a transaction considered tantamount to robbery. Thurland's Grove is literally 'a piercing' and refers to a natural feature as 'a gap in the land'. Former inhabitants of the village are remembered in the names of Bacon's Farm and Cottons's Corner, William Bacon was here in 1796 and Anthony Cotton in 1529.

The name of the Globe Inn features a simple image and suggests the place is open to all. However it should also be noted at one point it was used to represent Portugal and told prospective patrons Portuguese wines were on sale within.

Upwood

Recorded as Upwude in 974 and as Upehude in the Domesday census of 1086, this name comes from Old English *upp wudu* and tells us it was 'the higher woodland'.

W

Walsoken

This name is recorded as Walsocne in 974 and as Walsoca in 1086. Here the name comes from Old English *wall socn* and refers to 'the jurisdictional district near the Roman bank'.

The Bell is another reminder of the link between village pub and church, for centuries they were the only regular meeting places for the community.

Wansford

The earliest record of this name comes from 972 as Wylmesforda. Two possible Old English meanings for this name: 'ford by a spring' if this is from *wylm ford* or if this represents *waelm ford* this is 'ford by a whirlpool'. While the former does fit the record better, the meaning hardly makes it stand out and thus the alternative must be more likely.

Warboys

Listed as Weardebusc in 974, this is most likely from 'the bush of a man named Wearda', where the Saxon personal name is followed by Old English *busc*. Alteratively this may be *weard busc* and describe 'the bush affording protection', in which case this would be a look out or perhaps even an ambush point.

The White Hart first came to prominence as it was the image adopted by Richard III when he came to the throne. Later the name became the generic name for a pub, much as the vacuum cleaner is very often referred to as a 'hoover'.

Waresley

Domesday records this place as Weseresle and documented as Wereslea in 1169. Here is a Saxon personal name and Old English *leah* which tells us it was 'the woodland clearing of a man named Wether or Waer'.

Waterbeach

A name with its origins in Old English, originally from *becce* meaning 'valley stream'. To distinguish this place from Landbeach this place first added *ut* or 'outer' and was recorded as Vtbech in the Domesday record of 1086, later seen as Waterbech in 1237 with the addition of *waeter* or 'water'.

Locally we find the names of Bannalds, an unusual modern form of *bean healh* and describing 'the nook of land where beans are grown'. Joist Fen is even more corrupted, this being one of the few place names in England of wholly Latin origin, *jacitare* telling us it was the place where 'cattle are admitted to the forest' and would have been agreed to permit the animals there for a stipulated period of time. A third oddity is the name of Chalice Fruit, a local version of what seems to be *ceorl frythe* or 'the peasant's brushwood place'.

Other names are much clearer, such as Denny Anney from 'Dane's dry land in marsh', and Elmey Hill which is similiarly 'the dry land in marsh where elm trees grow', while Winfold Farm tells us it was 'the hollow where wolves are seen'. Individuals who have left their mark on the map include Thomas Adams, who was at Adam's Crossing by 1619, and earlier in 1279 Albric le Mason was associated with what is now known as Mason's Drive.

Pubs names are derived from signs, those began as simple advertisements for the product. These earliest signs were known as ale stakes, although not quite what the name suggests. Once anyone would brew their own ales and some would offer such to travellers. In order to advertise such it was pointless writing a sign, for they were likely as illiterate as the potential customer, hence a wayside tree would be cleared of its lower branches and a sheaf of barley tied to the trunk. Such an image became commonplace and when signs in the modern sense first appeared it was inevitable the product would feature prominently on many signs. One of the modern versions is that of the Brewery Tap. The Slap Up suggests a hearty meal is served here, the Sun Inn features the warm and welcoming image of the sun, and the White Horse is most likely a reference to the House of Hanover who ruled the nation from 1714 to 1837.

Waterbeach has revealed evidence of Roman habitation to the south of today's main body of houses. Archaeologists expected to find such as the village stands on Car Dyke, a Roman man-made watercourse which has been traced to Lincoln.

Wendy
Found in the Domesday census as Wandei, this is derived from Old English *wende eg* and describes 'the dry land in a river bend'.

Wennington
The earliest known record of this place name dates from 960 as Weningtone. Here a Saxon personal name precedes Old English *ing tun* and describes 'the farmstead associated with a man called Wenna'.

Wentworth
Domesday records this name as Winteuuorde when it was held by the Abbot of Ely. This is Old English *worth* preceded by an uncertain Saxon personal name, but is probably something akin to 'Wintra's enclosure'. Personal names are often the hardest to give with any certainty, not that these names were unknown but the large number of pet forms and nicknames make them well-nigh impossible to recognise.

Minor names here include Glover's Farm, which was home to Robert Glover by 1840. In the same year William Dunham was living at what is now the street named after him, Dunham's Lane. Granny's End Road is a corruption of the name of John de Granden, who was here by 1323 and who derived their surname from either Great Gransden or Little Gransden. Marroway Road tells us it was once a boundary marker for the name means 'the boundary way'.

Westley Waterless
Found as Westle in 1045, as Weslai in 1086, and as Westle Waterles in 1285, here is a name of Old English derivation. From *west leah* the basic name describes 'the westerly woodland clearing'. This is a fairly common name, hence the addition of *waeter laes* describing 'the wet woodland clearings'. Alternatively it may represent two names for the same place, rather than two very close places which have become a single settlement.

Hungry Hill is a derogatory name, created by neighbours to describe unproductive land or perhaps a comment on the skill of the farmers working it.

Weston Colville

Listings of this name include West tuniga geneara in 974, Westone in 1086, and as Westkoleville in 1324. Here is the common *west tun* or 'the farmstead to the west' and a place which came under the wing of one William de Coleville from 1203.

Minor names here include Mines Farm, a name derived from its association with John le Moyne who was here by 1272. Similarly William Quyting was at Whiting's Grove in 1236, while Chilly Hill still explains itself today.

West Water, The

As discussed under Old West River, this tributary of the Nene is actually older. However as this was already known by a name referring to its location it has not changed from 'the western water'.

Westwick

Seen in Domesday as Westuuiche, this name comes from Old English *west wic* and refers to 'the westerly specialised farm', almost always that speciality was dairy produce.

West Wickham

A name found as Wicchamme in 974, Wicheham in 1086, Quicham in 1267, and Whykham in 1317, this comes from Old English *wic hamm* and refers to 'the dairy farm of the hemmed in land'.

Burton End tells us it could be found 'above the tun or farmstead'; Streetly End is from *straet leah* 'the woodland clearing by the street' and was earlier known as Wool Street; Yen Hall was built on land associated with the *ean* or 'lambs'; Richard Cagghe was linked with Cadge's Wood by 1279; and in 1327 Thomas de la Hayr was linked with what is now known as Hare Wood. The White Horse shows this was a patriotic establishment in demonstrating support for the royal House of Hanover.

West Wratting

Found as Wreattinge in 974 and as Warantinge in 1086, here the basic name comes from Old English *wraett ing* and describes 'the place where crosswort or hellebore grows'. The addition distinguished this from another Wratting to the east.

Minor names here include Conger's Well, a name from Old English *cumb grafa* and telling of 'the well by the grove in the valley'. From *weard hlaw* comes the name of Wadloo Farms, a name meaning 'the look out hill'. Individuals who have contributed to the history of West Wratting are seen in the names of Chalice's Tree named after Stephen de Escahliers, Rand's Wood remembers John and William Randesson who were here by 1347, and William Scarlet was associated with Scarlett's Farm before 1441.

Whaddon

Domesday records this name as Wadone, a name which comes from Old English *hwaete dun* and describes 'the hill where wheat is grown'.

Hoback Farm tells us it can be found at 'the beck by a ridge spur'; Christ's College Farm was held by that educational establishment; and North Road Farm is on the Ermine Street, an alternative name for that Roman road.

Whittlesford

Despite this being 'Wittel's ford' and featuring the same personal name as the previous entry, there can be no suggestion these refer to the same person for they are thirty miles apart. Here the Saxon personal name is followed by Old English *ford*, giving a name recorded as Witelesforde in Domesday.

Ryecroft Farm does not tell us what was growing, this is 'the croft at the island' and reveals where it can be found'. Rayner's Farm was worked by James Rayner by 1769; The Quave is an unusual name, warning that here is a 'quaking bog', simply an unsteady surface; and Little Nine Wells certainly has a number of wells, although how many is difficult to say for certain as at least two are seasonal.

Hogshole is a local place name telling us of 'the hollow where hogs wallow'. The biggest clue to the origin of Dead Woman's Bush is the location on the parish boundary, an indication that the responsibility for burying the woman was disputed and this was the only solution. Perhaps she had committed suicide for apparently she was not permitted a burial in consecrated ground.

Another burial place is marked by the name of Clements Grave. Here records show a man named Clements hung himself in Drivers Barn and, as mentioned above, such were not permitted a burial in consecrated ground. Indeed most, as in this case, were buried at a crossroads for it was thought such unhappiness would continue into the next life and prevent the individual from finding peace in the afterlife. Hence burying them at crossroads was a way to keep them from roaming as, being confused by the number of roads, would not know which way to turn. This was certainly the case here for there is a written record of a witness telling how, with the coffin in the grave and a sod or two ceremoniously thrown on top, a stake was driven into the coffin, impaling the body, emerging below and rammed hard into the ground. This was supposed to ensure there was no chance of anything ever emerging from this grave.

The local here is the Bees in the Wall, a delightfully different pub name which would most likely have reflected bee-keeping. That the bees were 'in the wall' is no surprise, bee-keepers would often create an artificial hibernation cavity in a wall in order to prevent their precious colony from swarming elsewhere.

Whittlesey

With records of Witlesig in 972 and Witesie in 1086, this name features a Saxon personal name and Old English *eg* referring to 'the dry ground in marsh of a man called Wittel'.

Local names include those of Bassenhally Farm, Bassenhally Moor and Bassenhally Pits, all of which speak of 'the nook of land by the lime tree farm'. Canter's Doles comes from Middle English *cantour* and describes 'the precentor's endowment', a person who helped lead the congregation in worship (particularly in song) and who would have left an endowment of land for the benefit of the parish poor.

Eldernell describes 'the nook of land where alder trees grow'; Flegcroft describes 'the croft where sedge grows'; Funthams refers to 'the hemmed in land of the springs'; what was 'Laeter's *eg* or dry land in marsh' is now known as Lattersey; while The Lipneas is from 'Lippa's low lying land'.

People are remembered too, such as Henry Atkinson who were associated with Atkinson's Barn by 1650; Beale's Drove remembers the family of Mychel Beale, here by 1573; in 1276 John Brid was recorded here, although today his name has been corrupted to Bird's Hundred; Robert Cambers was at Camber's New Drove in 1840; the same year Richard Dearlove was recorded as living at Dearlove's Cottage; Drake's Farm was worked by Robert Drake by 1390; the family of Thomas Hughes gave a name to Hugh's Farm from at least 1840; Ives Drove is named after James Ives, here by 1600; Katie's Farm was home to the Keate family by the seventeenth century; and Richer's Drove was named after the family of Thomas Richer, here by 1381.

Public houses here include the Black Bull, an heraldic symbol which features in numerous coats of arms; the Bricklayers Arms shows how publicans would have had an earlier trade and possibly continued to supplement their income as a second trade. Until the trackbed brought the new mode of transport through here the Railway Inn cannot have existed. However surely the best pub name here is the Hero of Aliwal, a man who was actually born in Whittesley in 1787. Sir Harry Smith led the charge in the deciding battle of the Sikh Campaign (1846) at Aliwal in South Africa. So enamoured with the country was Sir Harry, that he moved to South Africa where he lived until his death in 1860.

What was once named The Bee was an unfortunate error for the name was originally the Letter B. This was not the only pub with this kind of name for there had also been pubs named the Letter A and the Letter C, both of which have now closed. Researchers have suggested there were once as many as fifty-two pubs open at one time here.

Wicken

Listed in Domesday as Wicha, this name comes from Old English *wicum*, a plural form of *wic* and describing 'the specialised farmsteads'.

Here Fodder Fen and Fodder Drove must indicate a place where rushes were cut, perhaps for fodder but surely for thatching too. America Farm is a remoteness name, that farthest flung finger of land which would have taken that much longer to reach. Howe's Farm was worked by John How before 1840, Gray's Farm was home to John de Grey from at least 1327, Hugo Dymmok gave the family's name to Dimmock's Cote by 1394, and Geoffrey de Sco Edmundo was associated with St Edmund's Fen by 1285.

Wilbraham (Great and Little)

Two places less than half a mile apart have a common origin in 'the homestead of a woman called Wilburh', where the Saxon personal name is followed by *burh*. Prior to the additions, which need no explanation, this place is recorded as Wilburgeham in 975 and as Wilborgham in 1086.

Oddly there are also two rivers with the same names – Great Wilbraham River and Little Wilbraham River being examples of back-formation.

At Great Wilbraham is Mutlow Hill which comes from *mot hlaw* 'the moot or meeting hill', Wilbraham Temple was a possession of the Knights Templar by 1226, and Shardelowes Well was associated with Edmund de Sardelowe by 1279.

Minor names at Little Wilbraham include Hawk Mill, from *halke myll* of 'the mill in the nook or corner of land'. Six Mile Bottom is named for it being a 'hollow six miles from Newmarket' in Suffolk. Well's Farm remembers Thomas Welle who was here by 1470, Corpus Christi Farm belonged to the famous college of that name by 1571,and Coventry Farm was given to Thomas Wale of Coventry in 1625 as a charitable donation to raise funds for that city.

The Carpenters Arms is a common pub name and, while the sign started showing the tools of the trade and more likely to be heraldic today the message is the same, the landlord had an earlier or alternative trade.

Wilburton

As with the previous name this features the Saxon name Wilburh, although there is no suggestion this refers to the same woman. Here the name is recorded as Wilburhtun in 970 and as Wilbertone in 1086, telling us of 'the farmstead of a woman called Wilburh'.

Minor names here recall those who were connected with the parish during its long history. Clarke's Lane was home to Edmund Clarke by 1840, in the same year William Martin was living at Martin's Way, by 1676 John Mingay was working Mingay Farm, and the family of William Mitchell were associated with Mitchell's Farm by 1523. Australia Farm does not feature a family name, this is a remoteness name given to that most distant corner of a parish.

Pubs here include the Kings Head Inn, showing this is a patriotic establishment. The Twenty Pence Inn takes its name from Twentypence Road, itself derived from the rental price put on the land here many years before it was ever developed. Note this is not modern decimal coinage, this is the old penny, when there were 240 pennies to the pound. Thus should the name perhaps be updated and renamed the Eight Point Three Three Pence Inn.

Willingham

Records of this name include Vilvlingeham in 1050 and as Wivelingham in 1086, this comes from a Saxon personal name and Old English *inga ham* and describes 'the homestead of the family or followers of a man called Wifel'.

Here the name of Crick's Farm is derived from former occupant John de Creke, who was here in 1298 and almost certainly originated from

Creake in Norfolk. Sneesby's Road is a lasting reminder of the family of Susannah Sneesby, here by 1745. Belsars Field is an Old French place name from *bel assis* or 'the beautiful seat', the lord of the manor thus reflecting on how pleasing he found this land.

Hempsalls Fen comes from 'the nook of Hefin'; Queen Holme is *cwene holm* 'the woman's dry land in the marsh'; and The Shoals reveals how wet this area was, this place was not dry for it means 'the shallows'. Long Shelfords, Short Shelfords, and Shelford's Farm share an origin from *sceolh ford* and tell us this was 'shelving land to the ford'.

The Stacks can be seen to be referring to 'the pile, heap', describing some sort of obstruction. Bourney's Manor Farm is named from a former tenant, either John de Brune from 1391 or Joan Burne in 1496. Crane's Fen, however, has only one potential source for the name, Robert Crane who was here in 1367.

One local is the Three Tuns, a tun being a large cask containing the equivalent of four hogsheads or 252 gallons. However here is specified the number three, which appears in the arms of the Worshipful Company of Vintners and Worshipful Company of Brewers. The Black Bull is a common name, one which may have heraldic connections or simply a rural image.

Wimblington

Documented as Wimblingetune in 975, here is a Saxon personal name and Old English *ing tun* and telling us of 'the farmstead associated with a man called Wynnbald'.

The Stitches is a local name referring to 'the pieces of land'; Lyon's Grove was home to William Lyon by 1797; while both Grays Farm and Grays Fen get their names from John Gray, here by 1826.

Naming a pub in the days when the vast majority of patrons were illiterate meant choosing a name was important as imagery was necessary to get across the message. It was also important that the image was fairly simple, for complex signs were expensive. Thirdly some consideration was given to both the location and potential custom. Hence the Anchor is a popular pub name, a simple image which has a clear link to the sea, while also being a religious image and a hope that one's faith will anchor an individual through life's storms.

Like most villages Wimblington has a war memorial remembering those residents lost in the two world wars. However here one name was removed when the memorial was refurbished and rededicated in 2005,

Wimblington Church

that of Percy Bush Cox. At the end of the First World War Percy was listed as 'missing in action believed dead', yet in 1950 he was reunited with his family. The local press covered the story, appearing alongside the memorial with his brother and father, pointing to his own name. Not long afterwards he committed suicide, when it transpired his absence had been quite deliberate and he had been living under the alias of Ernest Durham.

Wimpole

Domesday's record of Winepole shows this is 'Wina's pool', the Saxon personal name suffixed by Old English *pol*.

Former residents of the village who have left their mark on the minor place names include Richard and Stephen le Fraunceys who, in 1279, were living near French House, while by 1377 Geoffrey Cobbe was working what is now known as Cobb's Wood Farm.

Winwick

Found in Domesday as Wineuuiche, this name is derived from a Saxon personal name and Old English *wic* and meaning 'Wina's specialised or dairy farm'. Despite this featuring the same personal name as the previous entry there is no suggestion of these referring to the same person.

Wisbech

With only the notoriously unreliable record from Domesday as Wisbece, it is difficult to see exactly what this name refers to. While the eleventh century census is a great source of information, the different languages used by the Saxon tenants and the Norman surveyors make proper names difficult to interpret. While we know the origins are Old English, here this could be *wisc bece* and 'the marshy valley stream, *wisc baec* which would give "the marshy valley below the ridge', or perhaps the first element is the River Wissey, a river name referring to 'marshy stream'.

The Wisbech Canal is a name coined in the eighteenth century to refer to what had been the Wellestream before it was straightened. Wisbech St Mary takes the addition from the dedication of the church. Mouse Lane is derived from where the mouth of the Moreton's Leam was widened to prevent flooding, the name of the drainage ditch coming from its sponsor, Bishop Moreton.

Wisbech St Peter takes the dedication of the church; Crab Marsh describes 'the marsh where crab grass (or glasswort) grows'; Sibald's Holm gets its name from 'Sigbeald's marshland'; Bagdale Farm is a reminder of John de Bekedale, here by 1314; and in 1436 Thomas Heruy was associated with Harvey Field.

Newton is seen as Niwantune in 972, Neutone and 1213, this is clearly from *niwe tun* 'the newer farmstead'. Local names include Frank's Lane, named after John Frankes who was here in 1395; Folly Farm is from *fallow hoh* 'the yellow-ish nook of land'; Gaul Field is from *gafol feld* 'the open land subject to a tax or tribute'; Gull Field is 'the open land of the watercourse' from *gole feld*; Bradley's Bridge is a reminder of the family of Stephen Bridge, here in 1840; and Whirler's Hill takes the name of Reginald Whirler, here by 1327.

Street names here sometimes require little or no explanation, as in the case of Station Road, Railway Road, and Bridge Street. There are also the seemingly unimaginative names of First Avenue, Second Avenue, Third Avenue, Fourth Avenue, Fifth Avenue, Sixth Avenue, Seventh Avenue, and Eighth Avenue. Thankfully there is no room for a ninth or more.

Falcon Road is not named directly from the bird of prey but is derived from the Falcon public house being built here. Former clergymen who have left their mark on the town in the most obvious way in the form of street names include the Rev Henry Fardell, vicar of Wisbech and Canon of Ely, who is remembered by Fardell Road; Holmes Drive remembers the Rev William Holmes; King Street is after the Rt Rev G King, Curate of Wisbech; all of which will prove a lasting and more obvious reminder of these men of the cloth than any memorial.

Local families have also contributed to the street map. From the nineteenth century alone we find John Bellamy's family who proved the inspiration for Bellamy's Lane. James Cox and his family gave a name to Cox's Lane. Hall Road is derived from Thomas Hall and his family. Peckover Drive takes the name of the family who included William and Alfernon Peckover. Farm Henry Bird and his ancestors gave a name to Bird's Drove, as did the farming family of John Terrington to Terrington Close, and the family of grocer John Anderson to Anderson Close.

Hunchback Lane describes its shape and was probably named such well before any map included the name and thus already in local use for many years. Modern themes are seen in the names of Kingfisher Drive, Heron Road, Kestrel Drive, Redwing Drive, and Robin Mews. If a theme can be said to apply to just two roads then apples is that theme for Worcester Road and Bramley Road. The plant world also proved the inspiration for Laburnum Close, Lilac Close, Rowan Close, Jasmin Road and Wistaria Road, although sadly the wrong spelling was used for the final two examples.

Public houses here come from many areas. Some are obvious and need no explanation such as in the Wisbech Arms, Bowling Green, Bridge Inn, Horsefair Tavern, Locomotive, Market Inn, West End Inn, Blackfriars Free House, the Nene Inn, and the Woodman Cottage.

Imagery is all important in pub signs, the Wheel Inn, shows a wheelwright was nearby; at the Woolpack is a picture of the bale of wool for cloth-making weighing approximately 240 pounds; the Wheatsheaf was an heraldic image representing the Brewers' Company; the Three Tuns Inn copied the image used by the Worshipful Company of Vintners and the Worshipful Company of Brewers; the Red Lion most often represents Scotland; the Rose Tavern symbolising England.

Of course it was always a good idea to show support for the nobility. Here we find the Princess Victoria Country Inn, probably after the eldest daughter of Queen Victoria who married the German Emperor and King of Prussia, she died in 1901 just seven months after her mother. The

Queens Head is a general support for the monarchy; the Dukes Head would have been named after whomever was the hero of the day, most of the Duke of Wellington.

Religion is also well represented, some are quite obvious such as the Angel Hotel; or the Bell Inn; the Five Bells; the Flower Pot once contained lilies and represented the Virgin Mary, but the Puritans did not approve of such imagery and thus the name and image changed to a more subtle representation; and the Lamb and Flag shows this was a Christian premises, the lamb being the Son of God, and also a patriotic one; the Black Horse represented many families and bodies.

The Highwayman may have served the terrors of the coaching routes, although the name more often would have been chosen for its romantic imagery; the Hare and Hounds Hotel is a remnant from the days of the hunt; the Red Hart Inn features the great stag of the red deer, the best examples being truly splendid beasts; the Tydd Gate Inn takes the a local place name; the Railway Bell could not have been named before the new mode of transport came to Wisbech, the bell is reputed to have been rung to announce the imminent arrival of the next train; the Dun Cow is a simple rural sign; and the Clarkson Arms is named after the family of Thomas Clarkson (1760-1846), a renowned anti-slavery campaigner.

Wistow

Recorded as Wicstoue in 974 and as Wistov in 1086, this name comes from Old English *wic stow*. These elements are well known, however it is often difficult to know what these are describing. The element *wic* refers to a 'specialised farmstead', most often that speciality is dairy produce however here this may not be so. The element *stow* often proves difficult to define with any certainty, for it is used to mean 'assembly place', 'holy place', or simply 'place' and clarification is usually only by understanding the other part of the name or the history of the place. While it would be tempting to suggest this represents a special meeting place for religious or political purposes, we know of no other records suggesting same. Hence the most likely meaning is simply 'the place of the specialised farm', perhaps that speciality was a particular dairy product.

The local is the Three Horseshoes, a name which is more easily understood if seen as a question. Clearly a horse has four legs and requires four shoes, however they do wear out and are occasionally lost. Hence here the pub tells travellers there is a blacksmith available to look after the horse while the rider refreshes himself within.

Witcham

From Old English *wice hamm* this name speaks of 'the hemmed in land where wych elms grow'. This name is found as Wichamme in 970 and as Wiceham in 1086.

While Witcham Gravel clearly refers to an area where small stones abounded, other names are quite misleading. Hive Road would seem to indicate a place where bees were kept, however the true origin is quite different and of much greater significance for this tells us it was 'the road to the landing place' and thus where most of the goods were brought in and shipped out.

The local White Horse Inn shows an image associated with the royal House of Hanover. Witcham is the venue for the annual World Pea Shooting Championships every July

Witchford

No suggestion of any witchcraft here, this name comes from Old English *wice ford* and describes 'the ford where wych elms grow. The name appears in Domesday as Wiceford, when it was held by the Abbot of Ely indeed the last Saxon to hold this post was born in Witchford.

Many small communities refer to their local as the village pub, here this has been taken literally and the local is indeed named the Village Inn. Locals have also unofficially named the industrial estate the Rocket Base, for this was the original plan for the old RAF base which housed the 196 Squadron and their Vickers Wellington bombers, which was once due to become a missile base during the days of the Cold War.

Wittering

A name found as Witheringaeige in 972, as Witheringham in 1086, and as Witeringa in 1167, these forms seem to alternate between a suffix of *ham* 'homestead' and *eg* 'dry ground in a marsh'. It is tempting to offer the latter as Domesday's record of proper names can be unreliable. However the rest of the name is in no doubt, this comes from a Saxon personal name and Old English *ingas* referring to 'the *ham/eg* of the family or followers of a man called Wither'.

Woodditton

Here the name is found as simply Dictune in 1022, this comes from Old English *dic tun* and refers to 'the farmstead by a ditch or dyke'. Later we find the addition of *wudu* in a document of 1227 as Wodedittone, the 'woodland' distinguishes this place from Fen Ditton.

Derisley Farm comes from *deor leah* and describes 'the woodland clearing frequented by deer', although there is a possibility the first element is a personal name and thus 'Deor's woodland clearing'. The name of Camois Hall certainly features a personal name, this is a reminder of Ralph de Kameys, here by 1209.

Woodhurst

The earliest known record of this name is as Wdeherst in 1209, however we can still be certain the original name was simply Old English *hyrst* 'the wooded hill' with the later addition of *wudu* meaning 'woodland'.

Wood Walton

Found as Waltune in 1086 and as Wadewalton in 1200, this name originally spoke of 'the farmstead in a high forest' from Old English *weald tun* and later saw the addition of *wudu* or 'woodland'.

Woolley

Records of this name include Ciluelai in 1086 and as Wulueleia in 1158, where we can see how very different the Norman French idea of a Saxon place name can be, for this is certainly from Old English *wulf leah* and describes 'the woodland clearing frequented by wolves'.

Wyton

Found in Domesday as Witune and as Wictun in 1253, this name is derived from Old English *wic tun* and refers to 'the dairy farmstead'.

Three Jolly Butchers feature on the sign of the local pub, this name shows the local landlord often also served the community as the local butcher.

Y

Yaxley

This name is recorded as Geaceslea in 963 and as Iacheslei in 1086. Here the name comes from Old English *geac leah* and refers to 'the woodland clearing associated with a cuckoo'. It is well known this bird is migratory, spending more time away from our shores than it does here for it famously never rears its own young and thus can fly south much sooner than other birds. Hence it is possible this first element represents a personal name, probably a nickname.

At Yaxley we find a pub name which refers to a very specific skill. The Hatchet and Bill features the names of two tools used in hedging, the hatchet needs no explanation while the bill is short for bill-hook which has a long blade with a hooked or concave edge. The Duck and Drake refers to the wildfowl which would be seen on the nearby Holme Fens Nature Reserve.

Yelling

Seen as Gillinge in 974 and as Gellinge in 1086, this is a Saxon personal name with Old English *ingas* and describes the '(settlement of) the family or followers of a man called Giella'.

Common place-name elements

Element	Origin	Meaning
ac	Old English	oak tree
banke	Old Scandinavian	bank, hill slope
bearu	Old English	grove, wood
bekkr	Old Scandinavian	stream
berg	Old Scandinavian	hill
birce	Old English	birch tree
brad	Old English	broad
broc	Old English	brook, stream
brycg	Old English	bridge
burh	Old English	fortified place
burna	Old English	stream
by	Old Scandinavian	farmstead
ceap	Old English	market
ceaster	Old English	Roman stronghold
cirice	Old English	church
clif	Old English	cliff, slope
cocc	Old English	woodcock
cot	Old English	cottage
cumb	Old English	valley
cweorn	Old English	queorn
cyning	Old English	king
dael	Old English	valley
dalr	Old Scandinavian	valley
denu	Old English	valley
draeg	Old English	portage
dun	Old English	hill
ea	Old English	river
east	Old English	east
ecg	Old English	edge
eg	Old English	island
eorl	Old English	nobleman
eowestre	Old English	fold for sheep

Element	Origin	Meaning
fald	Old English	animal enclosure
feld	Old English	open land
ford	Old English	river crossing
ful	Old English	foul, dirty
geard	Old English	yard
geat	Old English	gap, pass
haeg	Old English	enclosure
haeth	Old English	heath
haga	Old English	hedged enclosure
halh	Old English	nook of land
ham	Old English	homestead
hamm	Old English	river meadow
heah	Old English	high, chief
hlaw	Old English	tumulus, mound
hoh	Old English	hill spur
hop	Old English	enclosed valley
hrycg	Old English	ridge
hwaete	Old English	wheat
hwit	Old English	white
hyll	Old English	hill
lacu	Old English	stream, water course
lang	Old English	long
langr	Old Scandinavian	long
leah	Old English	woodland clearing
lytel	Old English	little
meos	Old English	moss
mere	Old English	lake
middel ·	Old English	middle
mor	Old English	moorland
myln	Old English	mill
niwe	Old English	new
north	Old English	north
ofer	Old English	bank, ridge
pol	Old English	pool, pond
preost	Old English	priest
ruh	Old English	rough
salh	Old English	willow
sceaga	Old English	small wood, copse

Element	Origin	Meaning
sceap	Old English	sheep
stan	Old English	stone, boundary stone
steinn	Old Scandinavian	stone, boundary stone
stapol	Old English	post, pillar
stoc	Old English	secondary or special settlement
stocc	Old English	stump, log
stow	Old English	assembly or holy place
straet	Old English	Roman road
suth	Old English	south
thorp	Old Scandinavian	outlying farmstead
treow	Old English	tree, post
tun	Old English	farmstead
wald	Old English	woodland, forest
wella	Old English	spring, stream
west	Old English	west
wic	Old English	specialised, usually dairy farm
withig	Old English	willow tree
worth	Old English	an enclosure
wudu	Old English	wood

Bibliography

Barker, Anne. *Diaries of Whittleford*
Beris, Trevor. *Wisbech Hundred 1850*
Brown, James. *Gamlingay*
Dunkling, L. and Wright, G. *A Dictionary of Pub Names*
Dunn, Christopher. *The Book of Huntingdon*
Lamb, T. M. *Brampton Street Names*
Mills, A. D. *Oxford Dictionary of English Place Names*
Payne, Sara. *Down Your Street* Volumes I & II
Reaney, P. H. *Place Names of Cambridgeshire and Isle of Ely*
Reeve, F. A. *Cambridge*
Storey, Gertrude. *Culford Hall*
Tebbs, H. F. *Peterborough*
Tebbutt, C. F. *St Neots: History of a Huntingdonshire Town*

Also available from Sigma

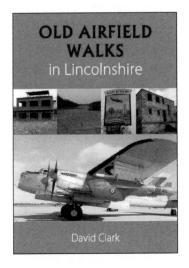

OLD AIRFIELD WALKS in Lincolnshire

David Clark

Old Airfield Walks in Lincolnshire
David Clark
Over 60 years after the end of the Second World War, Lincolnshire is still often referred to as the 'Bomber County', by virtue of the number of Bomber Command airfields once situated within its boundaries. The addition of Fighter Command, Coastal Command and United States Army Air Force bases made for a total of around fifty active airfields. This book comprises 20 circular walks centred on the remains of Lincolnshire's Second World War military airfields. Ranging from roughly 4 miles to 11 miles in length, the walks include additional features of interest and are supported by details of airfield history.
£8.99

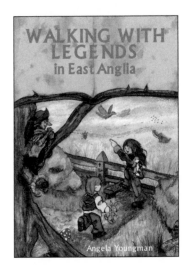

WALKING WITH LEGENDS in East Anglia

Angela Youngman

Walking with Legends in East Anglia
Angela Youngman
Walking is wonderful exercise and helps children become aware of the world around them. There are many places throughout the country which have stories, legends, history attached to them. By telling stories as you walk, and having related games and activities to play along the way, it can help overcome the problem of trying to get kids to walk just that bit further. Throughout this book focusing on the Norfolk, Suffolk and Essex, there are suggestions of areas that are good for walking, activities for along the way, and all have stories attached.
£8.99

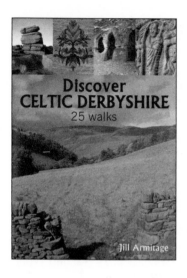

Discover Celtic Derbyshire
25 walks
Jill Armitage

Discover Celtic Derbyshire follows the Portway from the key Celtic Hillfort of Mam Tor in North Derbyshire to the Derbyshire/Nottinghamshire border at Stapleford and the southern river ports. Along the route, you will encounter the hermitages and industries, visit tribal hillforts, those iconic symbols of the age, and through megalithic mysteries, ancient feasts and festivals, discover the lifestyle of these people the conquering Romans considered barbaric. They were not. They had their beliefs and their gods and the Roman conquest of Britain did not signal the immediate death of Celtic culture. That is why this area has a treasure trove of early curiosities and customs, showing that pre-history is not quite dead in this ancient heart of England. Of the 25 walks in this book, 15 are circular, however, the route of the ancient Portway has been divided into ten manageable walks ranging from 3½ -7 miles.

All of our books are available through booksellers.
For a free catalogue, please contact:

Sigma Leisure, Stobart House, Pontyclerc
Penybanc Road, Ammanford SA18 3HP
Tel: 01269 593100 Fax: 01269 596116
info@sigmapress.co.uk   www.sigmapress.co.uk